Friends for Life

Friends for Life

Death Row Letters

Suzanne Michal
Robert Poyson #140419

First published by Dare To Expand, UK, in 2024

Copyright © Suzanne Michal and Robert Poyson 2024

All rights reserved. No portion of this book may be reproduced or transmitted in any form or by any means, electronic, graphic, or mechanical, including photocopying, recording, taping or by any information storage and retrieval system without the written permission of the author or Publisher, except in the case of short quotations used in critical articles and reviews.

The information presented is the author's opinion and does not constitute any health or medical advice. The content of this book is for informational purposes only. The ideas, suggestions, and exercises provided in this book are not intended as a substitute for seeking professional guidance. Neither the publisher nor the author shall be held liable or responsible for any loss or damage allegedly arising from the use or application of any suggestion or information contained in this book.

Cover design by Jason Lee Mitchell
Illustrations and symbols by Suzanne Michal
Drawings by Robert Poyson
Suzanne Michal's photograph by Jason Lee Mitchell
Robert Poyson's photograph courtesy of Robert,
taken by and inside death row with fake background

A catalogue record for this book is available from the British Library.

ISBN: 978-1-7394508-4-7 (hardcover)
ISBN: 978-1-7394508-2-3 (paperback)

To those who are contributing to make the world a kind, sustainable and harmonious place.

To my daughter and mom.

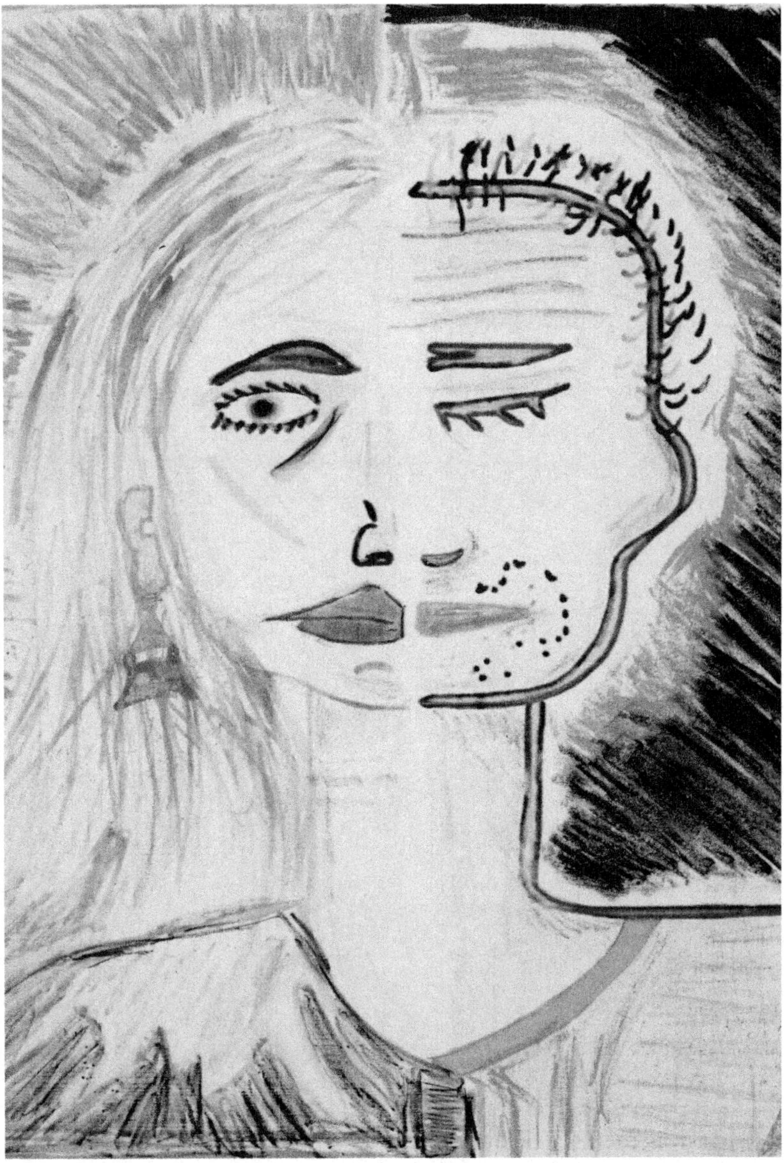

Contents

Foreword	xi
A Note to the Reader	xiii
Why this Book?	xv
Finding Each Other	1
Sharing Our Life Journeys	15
Reflecting on Our Friendship	191
Integrating the Murders	193
Who We Have Become	199
Friends for Life	217
Epilogue	*223*
Gratitude	*224*
Resources	*227*
Table of Illustrations and Drawings	*228*
About the Authors	*229*

Foreword

This is a remarkable book about a remarkable friendship. I have been hugely impressed and have been left emotionally and spiritually affected by it. The shared energy it conveys is extraordinary, and there is so much to absorb and reflect on. Suzanne and Robert's joint account is one of real significance.

Their connection is based around a searing honesty on both sides – an honesty that is possible only because of the instinctive trust established right from the beginning. Their correspondence develops at breakneck speed but remains respectful and free of any romantic overtones. All sorts of aspects and issues are raised as each writer is willing to take risks. In many cases this amounts to a psychic communion of a highly uncommon kind.

The two do not seek to place themselves in a flattering light; instead, they subject themselves to rigorous and often highly painful self-examination. Theirs is a shared journey; it is also one of equality and mutual respect.

Suzanne's personal journey is not just intertwined with Robert's but also has much to say to us in its own right. Hers, too, is a story of the ultimate resilience of the human spirit in adversity. This provides Suzanne with exceptional insight and understanding that underpins their relationship, especially Robert's involvement in a number of dreadful crimes that poses the most intense moral dilemma. His voice provides a powerful example of how someone condemned by society for terrible offences can nevertheless have so much value to contribute to us all. "Friends for Life" is his gift to the world.

One is left feeling that their two lives have come together as though there were some guiding hand. Their ongoing dialogue is life-changing and affirming, while in no way shying away from the darker side. Here is an outstanding example of the kind of "lifeline" on which the name of the organisation is based. A lifeline that allows people such as Suzanne to befriend a death row inmate. It has taken real courage on the part of both Suzanne and Robert to decide on the publication of their correspondence and write a book about their friendship. I can only commend it in the hope that others will be equally as astonished, moved and inspired as I have been.

Jan Arriens
LifeLines founder
25 October 2023

A Note to the Reader

We co-authored this book through our letter exchanges which took some creative juggling to say the least. It covers the first five years of our friendship and includes more than sixty of our letters. They have been kept in their original form, with only a few corrections for clarity and grammatical requirements. We selected the key ones, and some have been shortened. Their chronological order might sometimes surprise you. We have kept the original dates for each letter, but it could take two to five weeks for a letter to arrive. This reflects the nature of a friendship based on letter writing.

The names of the people mentioned have been changed to protect their privacy unless agreed.

We invite you, our reader, to set your own intention before you start. What do you want to gain from our stories and friendship? How far are you going to allow your heart to open?

Some parts of Robert's story might be upsetting to read and integrate, if so, place your hands on your chest and breathe.

Some parts of Robert's life might appear monotonous and repetitive, if so, place your hands on your belly and breathe.

Out of respect, we both ask you to refrain from looking on internet for information about Robert. First, hear his story narrated in his own words. Then research as much as you want.

As you read our letters, you will come across a symbol from time time, it is placed there purposefully for you to take a break and integrate. Gently smile, breathe, receive our gratitude.

Why this Book?

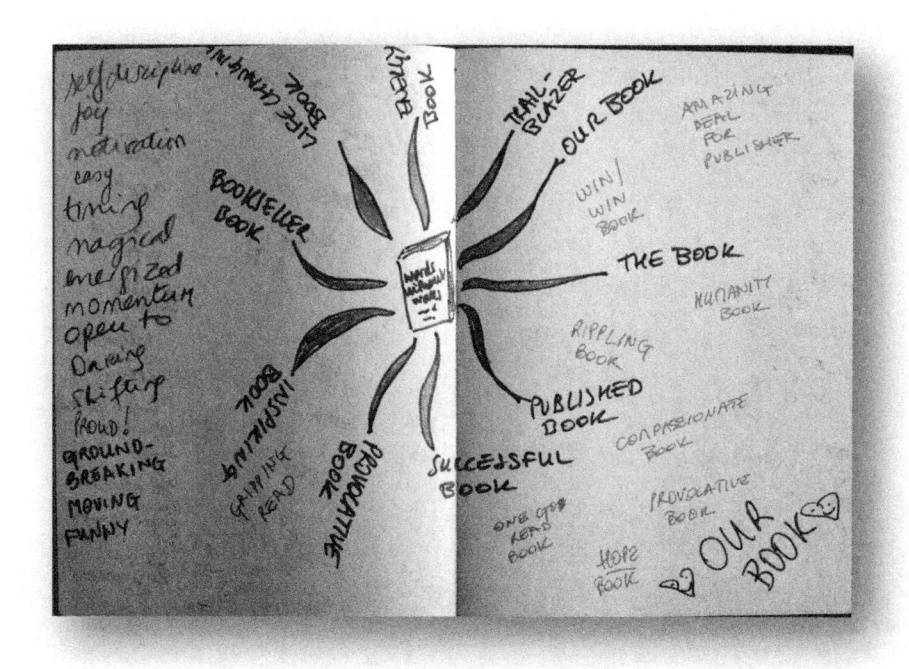

My desire to write this book emerged only a few months after getting to know Robert. I came to understand that our connection was unravelling something that could inspire others. Mostly, I felt completely powerless in front of Robert's solitary imprisonment and pending execution. I have no power to change American laws which maintain the death penalty and the reality of death row. I do not hold a magic wand which could change the karma of all involved with murder.

My level of helplessness reached such heights that, on one level of my being, I felt responsible for all forms of killing that exist. I rebelled against the death penalty present in a country that believes itself to be a leader of democracy. Robert had expressed his own feelings of frustration at not being able to contribute more to my life and society. So, instead of a magic wand, my solution came through the defying idea of us co-authoring a book. It took some time to dare suggest such a proposal to him but since he lives with a death sentence, I understand that time is precious and if our book was to be born one day, we had to act without delay.

In the past years we have witnessed many terrorist acts in the Western world, and it is easy to see who the victims are and feel compassionate, sad, or empathic towards them; yet it is far more difficult and less common to feel those same feelings towards a perpetrator. To label someone a murderer describes their acts, however it does not describe who they are as a person, nor does it allow us to understand their story that brought them to perpetrate their actions.

My intention is to shatter preconceived ideas about a real murderer and show the power of friendship. Our story is not a fiction—Robert is a real person like you and me. I am inviting you to break the taboo of befriending a murderer through my friendship with Robert.

In our society we receive important information, messages and teachings from different types of people, but rarely does it come from the voice of someone who is imprisoned on death row and facing execution. This book delivers powerful messages from someone who does not normally have a voice.

Robert's humanity struck me from the first letter I received from him. My openness was put to the test. I felt challenged and enriched by his transparency in showing me his true self, even the darkest corners of his childhood, his acts of murder and his encaged life on death row.

When we hear Robert speak through his letters, we are provoked to go beyond our judgements, preconceptions, beliefs or fears and see a human being beyond his acts and find a deeper level of empathy we maybe did not know we were capable of.

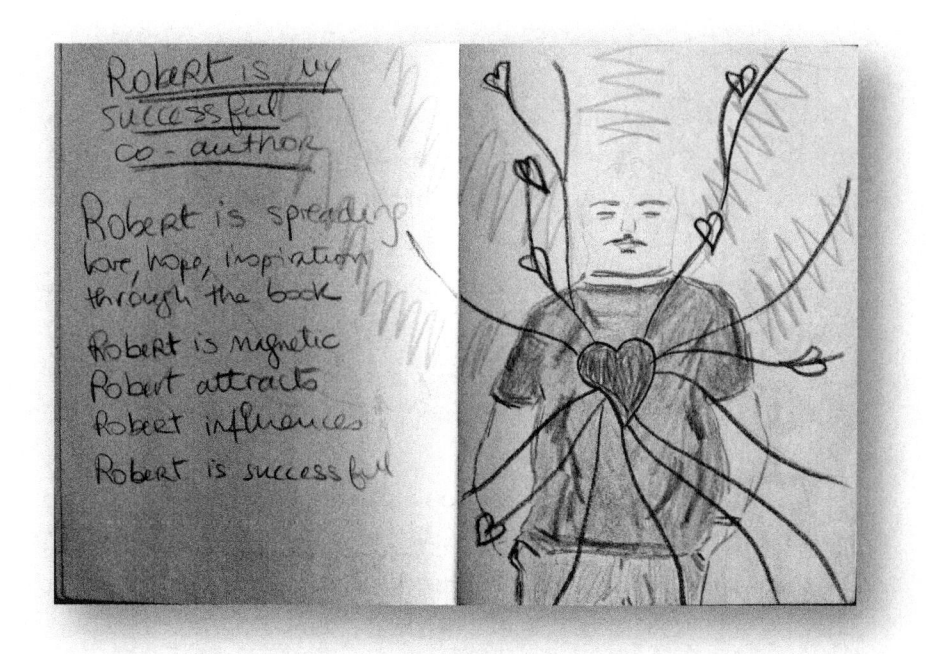

As a convicted murderer sentenced to death, I have constantly heard the myths that people on death row are the worst of the worst, that the death penalty is a deterrent to murder and many other falsehoods. The reality is easier said in a phrase that someone once shared with me: "Nobody should have their whole life judged by their worst moment".

Death rows around America are full of people who made terrible mistakes, but mistakes that, as some politicians say, can be "rehabilitated". It is a matter of showing us that regardless of our past, we are worthy of being loved.

During my nineteen years on death row, I have met people through letter writing who have wanted to get to know me. But it is not until I met Suzanne that I realized what it meant: "Getting to know me".

How could I let people know me if I myself didn't know who I was, if I didn't know that I was worthy of love and of loving myself. I am not talking about romantic love but a deeper meaning of what the word carries.

I hope that as you read this book you are able to get to know yourself and that it will give you the strength to deepen your own journey of self-discovery. May our experiences help you, our reader, realize more that you are worthy of receiving love from others but most importantly from yourself. I see you spreading this force from one person to the next.

I believe the only way for us as a civilization to truly grow and evolve is to love ourselves and others, love our surroundings and our so-called "enemies".

My intention in writing this book is to show that we can help our planet and ourselves heal by living the power of kindness. My friendship to Suzanne has taught me this lesson. Through her kindness I have been able to grow as an individual and as a spiritual being.

Suzanne is a strong and amazing soul, a woman who has overcome many obstacles and expanded her mind. She has shown me all the willingness and patience needed in getting to know a person whom most of society discards as not worth saving. She looks beyond the prejudice in the world and the scare tactics many governments use.

I believe we all can learn something from Suzanne—her stories, wisdom, and free-spirited ways of looking at life. Her voice in this book can teach us how to be more loving, curious, open and connected to our spiritual nature. She has been like a teacher to me and opened my mind to the importance of making peace with others and myself. I hope you can be as transformed by Suzanne's aliveness as I have been.

Finding Each Other

In order to fully grasp the significance of the beginning of my friendship with Suzanne, you must know that a year before we met in 2015, I had received a letter from Lifelines asking me if I was interested in having a new pen pal. Due to my appeal process and pending execution, I had decided not to write to someone new. It wouldn't have been fair to anyone to begin a friendship when there was limited time.

Then miraculously, in March 2014, the court of appeals granted me a relief in favour of another guy here on death row. My appeal was frozen. My lawyers were optimistic.

As I thought about the possibility of my court case taking a few more years, I decided to reply to Lifelines and let them know that I was interested in meeting someone new. I did ask that it be a female and someone over thirty-five years old because it was more likely that we'd have common interests. In my experience the younger crowd tends to be busy and less reliable at letter writing. I was told that when someone became available, they'd pass my information along. So, I waited and began to try and figure out what my future entailed.

At last, in February 2015 I received a letter from England. I looked at the envelope and it didn't have a return address. I thought "no problem" because sometimes people put their address at the end of their letter. So, I read the letter. It sounded down to earth, it brought a smile to my face and filled me with energy because from the beginning Suzanne was looking at me as a human being, not as a criminal.

She was straightforward and honest. I saw a person I knew I had to reach out to and find out more. Then the heartbreak, no address at the end of the letter and the thought came into my mind: Too good to be true. I put her letter at the end of my bed and sat back. About an hour later, I reread it and looked inside the envelope for an address but nothing.

Over three weeks I thought about the letter and by the second week in March, I received another one from this woman who had captured my mind. I am a romantic and tend to fall in love too quickly but with Suzanne, it was different, she intrigued me, she had made me already think.

I automatically looked for an address on her second letter but there wasn't one. I thought it was a cruel joke, that somehow, something got lost but as I read the letter, I knew it couldn't be a joke because why would this woman be sharing personal information about herself with me. This wasn't a cruel joke! But I still didn't understand why she didn't send her address. So, I wrote to my Lifelines coordinator and asked her if she could find out what was going on. I also included a letter for Suzanne and a little hello card I had drawn.

When I finally received a response from Suzanne, I could see how much my letter had meant to her. It was great to see her original reaction and I could actually feel her emotions. I could see that she was inexperienced in writing to someone on death row. There was a type of innocence about her response. But in that innocence, I could feel her honesty and willingness to open up.

I began to see that the extent of her spirituality was beyond my own and for a brief moment I got scared. Scared that I wasn't experienced enough. Scared because in my spiritual beliefs I was strong but to actually sit down and describe them was difficult. I knew what I felt, I knew what I believed but I did not know how to share it. Because I could not describe my spirituality, I was afraid that Suzanne would think I was fake and decide that I wasn't worth writing to.

I was drawn to her because I knew she could teach me so much. I needed this as I was preparing myself for my next life and for my execution at some point. Feeling Suzanne's openness, I knew she would be important in my evolution and could help me. I felt that meeting Suzanne was part of a bigger plan. It started with a mysterious and what seemed like a too good to be true one-off letter.

In my late teens, my mum took me to the cinema to see a documentary about a man on death row who got executed. This film impacted on me, big way.

I still hold vague sensations of certain images: grey cells and corridors. The colour that remains in me is a cold, barren grey. I especially remember the execution room. It felt like an extremely controlled space where feelings are absolutely forbidden, where solely automatic gestures and movements are to be performed. It seemed so foreign to me, resembling a place where aliens experiment on humans in a science fiction film.

The inmate shared that he had pen friends and how much it helped him in his torturous solitude. As a sensitive girl, I was deeply touched in my heart and soul. The coldness of that story must have disturbed me to the point of knowing that one day I too would give my friendship and warmth to a person who found himself or herself in that situation. I knew that at some point in the future I would write to someone on death row.

This seed of certainty got planted so deeply in my being that it took over three decades of gestation before it started warming up and eventually germinate. It happened when I came across an advert in a magazine for the organisation Lifelines. I was struck by their logo of a dove flying towards outstretched hands through bars. The buried seed received a nudge, a shove. Lifelines puts people in touch with inmates on death row in the United States to become their pen friend. I noted the organisation's details somewhere, but they ended up buried under the busyness of my life.

From time to time, I did come across that name and logo and I would play in the background of my awareness with what those words "lifelines" meant or could potentially mean. The words played silently with my soul: life lines, writing lines for life, life as a line, life as a lifeline, the line of life, lines of life...

This word play lingered and faded as I was too preoccupied dealing with being a single mum, juggling full-time jobs to part-time jobs, health issues, exhaustion which led to the chronic illness M.E., bereavements, longing for a loving partner. You get the picture of my then life! Hence, writing to someone on death row remained on the back burner and I never took any action.

However, in the summer of 2014, I finally wrote on my to-do list: contact Lifelines. At the time I was facing the possibility of going through a major operation and I expect this was making me consider my mortality and unfinished businesses like writing my will. Well, some people die during or after an operation, no? Since being a mum, I had considered doing a will many times but consistently avoided it. So off I went and wrote my will! That was a big one, putting in concrete how I would like my daughter to be taken care of after my potential death and what would happen to my belongings. It placed peace into my mind and soul.

Writing to someone on death row was another more elusive action I needed to act upon to feel I was aligned with my inner self in case I died from that dreaded operation. Maybe it was also the fact that suddenly I had tons of spare time as I could not do much with my giant belly full of two uterine grapefruit size fibroids and numerous apricot and cherry size ones. Maybe I felt I needed to fill up that time with some meaningful actions which were not too demanding for my body. I trust it was a mixture of many factors.

Once I decided to finally take action it only took five tiny minutes! I went on the internet, typed Lifelines UK, found their contact details and sent a short email about my interest in becoming a member. The seed sprouted its first leaf in literally a spark of a moment after some thirty odd years of gestation.

I now understand how there is a timing for such actions and events to take place, like when one falls in love, prior to that there is a succession of tiny junctures chained perfectly together for the meeting to happen. Contacting Lifelines was one of those timing things.

After sending the email I felt almost saintly good. It was simple and banal, an email amongst so many other ones and yet it felt gigantic. There was a sweet and peaceful relief in this tiny act. I felt more aligned to my integrity. The next day I received a polite and professional reply, thanking me for my interest and notifying me that they could send me more information by post. And so, a couple of weeks later, I received a big envelope filled with the organisation's quarterly magazine, brochure, membership Sign Here type documents.

I froze. The reality of murderers, death row, isolation, executions, was not rosy after all. It repelled me to be frank. Was I being attracted to drama? Why on earth would I want to connect with a murderer? It suddenly felt perverse. Did I have an unconscious need for trauma? I simply went from excitement to rejection in a matter of seconds. I could barely touch the magazine with my hands without feeling a sense of alienation from the people on death row. I struggled to read their articles and poems. I could not even look at their magnificent drawings. I could not come close to their humanity and sensitivity expressed beautifully.

It felt foreign to my reality, too extreme for my sense of well-being. I suddenly realised that maybe, I was not as interested in writing to an inmate as I had believed. I sensed that it would shake me out of my comfort zone. I did not like it. I had been shaken enough in the past. This time, I even had to pay for it, only fifteen pounds a year, mind you, but still. It felt absurd. The invitation to become a Lifelines member had turned hostile.

I took the safest road, and all those papers went into a drawer. My emotional reaction went simmering, yet again, in the pit of my mind where I had to find important answers to questions such as: Could I connect to someone who has killed? How can I befriend someone who is going to be killed in a rational, controlled, and structured manner by the very people who are punishing him or her for the same act of killing? How would I react if my pen "friend" is aggressive or unpleasant?

Trust was an underlying issue and it made me question if I was going to give my name or address? In short, how can one trust someone on death row? How would I know if he or she tried to manipulate me into thinking that they were a nice person? And what if my pen friend is a man? This also triggered a slight unease in me: I wondered if his aim in writing to me would be to fall in love, maybe go sexual on paper. Yes, I did feel uneasy there. I was not interested in falling in love with a guy on death row nor was I interested in getting horny in letters!

This inner simmering gently bubbled for roughly six more months. At times, I felt like unearthing that blasted seedling with its one leaf and proclaim loudly and proudly "No way, I am not going to write to someone on death row. Thank you very much". It felt easier to shut down what seemed now a stupid and naïve idea.

However, my teenage calling to befriend an inmate proved to be the strongest of us two. I could not get rid of the seedling. The quest to answer my questions was being battered around. I would push it down from my conscious mind into my subconscious where it could be dealt with. Ignorance can be bliss.

I did not notice when and how my simmering questions all got answered, but somehow, they did, and I started to feel more positive and safer about Lifelines and death row. My heart had opened up. My fears and resistance settled: pampered, and reassured that it was not a mad endeavour but more an altruistic, yet original journey I was embarking on.

By early December, after having refused to have a hysterectomy for a year, I no longer had a choice but to have open surgery into my uterus. I looked six months pregnant. The pressure and discomfort in my lower back and other organs grew literally day by day. I even struggled to pee. I embarked on a slow process of preoperative hospital appointments. Then miraculously, I received a second email from Lifelines asking me if I still wanted to join. That administrator was truly inspired to email me again after so long and dare check if I still was game. I am grateful for her pro-activity. The timing was perfect as I was done with my introspection and was at peace with becoming a Lifelines member. My answer to that email was a bright open "Yes, I want to do this. Now is the time. Let me do it".

Within a few days, my Lifeline coordinator rang me to let me know about my pen friend to be. I found myself on the phone, engaged in a pretty surreal conversation. I felt a bit like an adoptive parent who receives for the first time a list of data about their child to be: gender, origin, a kind of brief to let you know that this person is really about to enter your life.

My pen friend was a man called Robert, of American and Mexican origin, fluent in Spanish and English in speaking and writing. He described himself as not religious but spiritual to which I had to smile as this tiny piece of information resonated with my core. He had been on death row for eighteen years. She told me that I could go on the prison's website to see a photo of him and read about the charges against him. This did not resonate with me at all. I felt that if one day I was to know why this man found himself where he was, I would learn it from him, through his own words, in his own rhythm and most importantly not before contacting him.

I now know that if I had found out the details of his murders before writing my first letter, I would have firmly closed the Lifelines chapter out of my life. I would have sealed my doors shut, hermetically. My intention was to connect to him as a person beyond his acts of killing. That was my respect to him and I am glad I handled it that way.

I knew that I was not entering a casual friendship. I can fantasise about Robert getting a life of imprisonment, but this would still be no natural context for any fellowship. I felt committed to befriend Robert unconditionally, regardless of whether he was going to drive me crazy, disappoint or make me angry. I felt committed to write to him until either he or I would die. I somehow trusted we would co-create between us ways to make our friendship live, unless we both decided to stop it for whatever reason.

Now, I want to confess a little secret. Secretly, deep inside of me, I was hoping that my level of commitment to Robert would create the karmic cause for me to be able to attract and commit to a man: the love of my life.

In early January 2015, I wrote my first letter to Robert. What does one write in a first letter to an inmate on death row? I yearned to be myself as much as I could. I wanted to show Robert my true self. I wanted radical honesty and transparency to be the foundation for our communication and friendship. Why else would I want to connect with someone under those circumstances? After all, I was writing to someone on death row, so his death is never far away. I was going to make friends with a man whose future entails his potential execution, and his past includes murdering, but I was not going to censor myself because I am "free" and he is "encaged".

Pretending, hiding or lying simply don't work for me. I wanted the freedom to express anything and everything to Robert as it emerged.

I was aware that radical honesty is not a widespread way of sharing with others. It can be perceived as blunt, aggressive or defensive. So, I knew I would have to wrap it in kindness and respect. Of course, I had no certainty whether Robert would feel the same.

In fact, I took great pleasure in writing my first letter. I felt alive and creative like a little girl. I did not have to think much about what to share. It felt spontaneous, like a free-flowing dance between the page and my pen.

Later, when I posted the letter, I was intrigued to see if the lady at the post office counter would notice the address and that I was writing to someone in a prison in the United States. But she acted as if everything was normal and maybe it was!

My Lifelines coordinator had explained that it can sometimes take time for an inmate to reply as they might have issues around trust or opening themselves despite their longing for a friendship. So, in a way, I held a kind of blind faith that one day, when the time was right, I would receive a letter from my pen friend. It did not bother me to wait for his first letter.

I even wrote a second letter quite quickly after the first. I did not receive a response from Robert for quite a while and soon it dawned on me that I had not given him my address or the address of our coordinator. I had assumed he knew to send his letters through her first. Funnily enough, at about the same time, I received an email from our coordinator informing me that Robert had written to her because he did not know where to reply.

I had innocently relied on Lifelines to tell him where to write to. I realised I had to take one hundred percent responsibility for writing and engaging with a death row inmate, nobody else, not even Lifelines would, nor could take any responsibility for the door I was opening.

When I finally received Robert's first letter, I was sitting on my sofa, in a weakened, raw and shaken state from the operation. I opened a white A5 envelope with my own handwriting in purple ink, the one I had previously posted to our coordinator for her to forward my mail. When I opened it, in a state of indiscernible emotions, I found an unusual long white envelope, bearing a round American postal stamp, and an exceptionally neat handwriting forming my name C/O Lifelines address.

On the left top hand side of the envelope, it stated the pre-printed sender's address in capital letters: INMATE MAIL: DEPARTMENT OF CORRECTIONS, his inmate number (yes, Robert goes by a number!), another number which I later learnt to be his cell, the name of the prison, the name of his prison unit, a P.O. Box number, a city name, an American state, USA. With the additional prison note "for International Use Only."

All that information and those numbers gave me a shock. They put a definite context to where his letter had come from: a bunker of imprisonment and punishment.

I sat on my sofa motionless, quite incapable of even understanding what I felt, quite amazed really. So many emotional contradictions and complexities, so much joy and anticipation at witnessing the birth of a new friendship, our budding association.

Finding Each Other

Sharing Our Life Journeys

30th January 2015

Dear Robert,

Hola! Como estas? Me llamo Suzanne y yo bibe in London Inglaterra. I think this is the limit of my Spanish!

I am writing to you sitting and facing the winter English sun which is surprisingly very warm through the window. A real treat and a real change from grey London winters.

So, here I am, connecting with you through Lifelines. I am really excited about doing this and getting to know another fellow human being living on this blue planet whilst you get to know me.

I knew when I was fifteen years old or around that age, that I would one day befriend someone on death row as I saw a documentary about an inmate who got executed and it touched me. Well, in two weeks, I am going to be fifty years old. It is never too late.

I am so glad that you define yourself as spiritual but not religious as I am the same.

I am half French and half Scottish. I have lived in sunny (today) London for the last eleven years with my daughter who is sixteen years old and our cat Couscous (black and white). I am a bit of an original woman I suppose. A bit of an artist.

My family lives in France, Germany and in Haiti in the West Indies. I have to let you know that in two weeks I am seeing a surgeon as I need surgery. So at some point in the next month or so I might not write as I will be in hospital and then recovering.

I actually love writing and nowadays, nobody writes letters to anyone. So, I am happy to have found you to write to and receive letters from! I thank you in advance.

OK, this is letter number Uno! I am really looking forward to read from you whenever the fancy takes you.

Take care. Kindly,

Suzanne

March 1st 2015

Hello Suzanne,

How are you doing? As for me I am doing good. I received your letter dated January 30th a few weeks ago and wanted to respond. I am sorry that it has taken a while for me to respond. Your letter didn't have a return address and so I had to write to Lifelines because I was confused.

Well, I guess I should say hi and that it is an honor to meet you. From your letter I am assuming that our coordinator gave you the introduction I sent to her when I requested the help in finding me a friend to write to.

I must say that your Spanish or the limits of it :-) are good though there are some spelling errors. I was able to understand you and the words were arranged in the right order, this tends to be difficult to do for most.

Your reason for wanting to write to me is very moving. I am curious as to the name of the movie you watched when you were young that touched you so much and made you want to write to someone on death row. You are right, it is never too late to start writing.

In 2008 I quit looking for people to write to because I was about to get married to a woman I met via another pen pal organization and I was writing long letters two or three times a week to her. I felt it wouldn't be fair to others because I wouldn't have much time. I got married in 2009, but in late 2010 things fell apart and by 2011 we split up. I am currently waiting for divorce papers. As you'll see I am a little rusty at letter writing.

I had to smile at your words about getting to know another human being on this blue planet. It will be great to get to know you. I am excited at this possibility. I do ask only one thing, if I say something that offends you please tell me. Honesty is the best way to build a friendship and I know that I have a tendency to stick my foot in my mouth. Please feel free to ask any question. I am open to any conversation you want to have.

As for me being spiritual, I have nothing against religion. I have my opinion on it, but my beliefs tend to lean towards Buddhism, although I am not a Buddhist.

As for my surname, I have heard before that it is French or almost French. Some guards tend to say it the French way. I can only say that it was a name chosen by my grandfather and his two brothers. They were orphans and lived in an orphanage. They changed their surname when they got out. Why they chose it no one can tell me but this is my name. It is fun to hear all the pronunciations.

I am sorry to hear you are going to need surgery. I do hope it will all turn out good and I do understand that you'll need time to recover. Write when you can.

There is nothing wrong with your description of yourself as being an original woman and a bit of an artist. It is good to know that there are still original people out there. Nowadays, everyone tends to be like lemmings, especially here in the US. I am curious, may I ask in which way you are a bit of an artist?

It is good to know you have a 16 years old daughter. I have a 17 years old daughter who will be 18 in May. I have to shake my head in disbelief every time I say it. I can't believe it. Anyway, I hope all is well with your daughter.

Let me say, it is I who should thank you for writing. Receiving letters in here is a way to escape even if it is only for 10 to 15 minutes to read your letter and then the time to write back. I don't have to think of this place then. So thank you. I hope that we are able to become friends and that our personalities don't clash. This is often one of the reasons people quit writing. I hope all works out.

I will usually write back after I get a letter in the next day or two and if for some reason you don't get a letter, it is the mail. I am very punctual about writing or at least I try to be.

Well hey Suzanne, I guess, I better close here for now so that I don't bore you too much :-). I hope to hear from you soon. Until then, take care of yourself, be safe and good luck with your surgery.

Best wishes, Robert or Bob

> Well hey Suzanne, I guess I better close here for now so that I don't bore you too much 😊. I hope to hear from you soon so until then take care of yourself and be safe and Good luck with your surgery.
>
> Best Wishes
>
> Robert
>
> or
>
> Bob

Sunday 22nd February 2015

Hi Robert,

Early on a winter morning, the sun is shining bright, the roofs and grass are all white, covered in frost. It is beautiful to say the least. I am about to listen to a great coaching program which I have been doing for the last two weeks but I feel like writing to you first. Bueno.

I finally have a date for my operation in three weeks. I am very relieved as I am in pain and discomfort all the time. Hurrah! The solution is in less than one month now. I can't wait. It is a bit scary at the same time. I have never had an operation before.

By the end of May, I shall go back to work. I am an Assistant Manager in a charity shop and self-employed as a holistic therapist.

I am not quite sure what to share with you this morning. I expect, I am a bit flat.

I spent the day yesterday at my friend's Chaz and her mum Bella. Bella is a good friend of mine. She is dying and in palliative care. I saw them both which was really nice, and we watched the film "The Theory of Everything" about the life of Stephen Hawking. Maybe you know him. He is an English astrophysicist (a man in his seventies now) who has gone as far as the human mind can into time and space. His body is completely paralysed, and he can't even talk. When he was 22 years old, he was told he had a degenerative illness and would only live two years. He can move a bit of one finger, and this is how he operates his computer which speaks for him. An incredible true story of the human spirit. Within his paralysed body, he became one of the most important minds in the history of mankind.

Do you like to read? Do you have access to books and films? I would love to learn about your life. Everyone's life is precious. I was a practising Buddhist for 19 years but now I am simply aware of our spiritual nature. It feels good.

Mi amigo Robert, ti cartera amiga Suzanne de London Inglaterra!

Kindly,
Suzanne

March 8th 2015

Hello Suzanne,

How has everything been going? As for over here I am doing well. I received your letter last night and wanted to sit down and respond to you. It was great to hear from you.

I am hoping that this letter gets to you before your operation. I know it will be scary going in but just think of it as the beginning of a new life with no more pain and discomfort. I do hope it all goes well and that I will hear from you soon.

I was sorry to hear about your friend who is dying. I do know of Stephen Hawking.

Well, first let me say that my life wasn't the greatest. There was a lot of physical, mental and sexual abuse when I was growing up. The physical and mental were by stepfathers or boyfriends of my mom. The sexual was by a close family friend. I never knew my biological father until after I was locked up in here. From age 11 to 19, I was in and out of young offenders' institutions, or on the streets. I was into drugs and gangs. I burnt a lot of bridges with my family.

I was arrested for the murders in August 1996, days after turning 19. I was sent to the row November 1998 and have been here since. For a long time, since I have been on death row, I blamed everyone else. Not until about 2005, did I finally start to look at the true culprit: myself.

This is just the basic outline of my life. If you have any specific questions about anything, I have told you, you can ask. I am honest and open, or at least I try to be. If there is a question, I can't answer I will let you know.

How about you? What was your life like?

I am able to get books from the library once a week which I try to take advantage of every week. I read pretty much whatever I can get my hands on. I do read more of the paranormal realm of literature. My favourite author is Jean M. Auel. She wrote the Children of the Earth series and I have read the whole series many times. I try to re-read it once a year. We can get books sent in but because of constant rule changes it is just too much of a hassle, so I just read from the library.

We do get TV in our cells, we are allowed a 13 inch screen but we only get cable channels and four prison channels where they show educational programs. My favourite movies are "Contact" starring Jodie Foster, "Time machine" and "The Underworld" series with Kate Beckinsale. I don't watch too much TV. It just depends on how I am feeling that day.

Well, I guess I better close here so I can get this out. I hope all is well and this letter finds you in good spirits. So until I hear from you, take care and be safe.

Tu amigo Robert.

13th March 2015

Hi Robert or Bob! :-)

First, my apologies, it is only after I posted to you the Lifelines magazine that it dawned on me that you did not have my address! Or I assumed Audrey, our coordinator, had given it to you or I just felt so at ease writing to you that it did not cross my mind. I am also fully taken by my body's distress at the moment. So, there you are. I have learnt now.

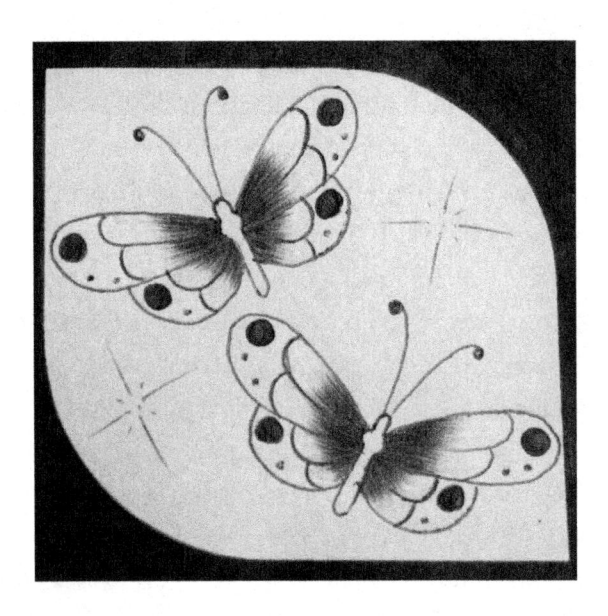

I have received your first letter and gorgeous hand drawn card with your generosity of good wishes inside.

I am lost for words to explain what it did to me to read your letter and be the recipient of your artistic skills. It felt like such a "normal" letter as if you lead a "normal" life but then you mention the guards and "this place". I was fascinated by the inmate entry on the envelope and this really broke the "normality" of your letter. If you see what I mean!

I have decided to write this letter over several days so that I post it closest to when I have my operation. So much I want to say but my pen is slow on the paper. Your words on your card "remember to smile" are so perfect as I tend to smile a lot. This is also going to be my motto for when I go under the anaesthetic because I want to smile as soon as I regain consciousness afterwards. So, 100% spot on from you. I put your card on my chest of drawers in my lounge, next to my little OM statue that my brother gave to me. You know the Buddhist chant of the universal sound OM.

Under this OM statue, there is a little piece of white paper and on it I had written your full name. The first time I heard your name I emotionally wrote it down. After the phone call ended with our coordinator, I placed this tiny piece of paper under this great symbol of universal life force: OM. Your name is still there but now your card is next to it.

Well? Who is the artist? You it seems or us two. My daughter Scarlet was amazed at the quality of your art.

What is your daughter's name? Scarlet's birthday is also in May. Does your daughter come and visit you?

I am sitting on my sofa which is a light purple colour, still in my pyjamas (it is 8.30 am), I have incense burning, outside it is a typical grey winter London day, my garden's grass is purple as it is covered with violet flowers. It's stunning. Here is one for you. They smell lovely too. I am not sure that the colour will stay under the Sellotape but there you are. A bit of my garden is flying to you in the USA. My cat has just gone outside through her cat flap. Soon, I shall do my morning meditation.

Your handwriting is very neat. I hope you can easily read mine. Plus remember I am French so my written English can be a bit funny. :-)

Onto getting to know each other: I thought that maybe we could write chronologically about our lives. What do you think?

For sure, we will share things that are easy and others that are not. That's life. Thank you for making me at ease in telling me that I can ask you anything. I am like you: sometimes too direct, too honest or too radical. If I too offend you, please do say so. Thanks for sharing that in your letter.

I don't know what the name of the documentary I saw all those years ago was. I hate the name death row. It is awful. How do you call where you are? You have said "that place". It would be useful if you could describe to me where you are and a typical week. I would get a better understanding of your life. I can do the same if you want.

I am fascinated by the story of your granddad and his brother. Courageous men it sounds. Did you know them? Their name is Mexican? Where were you born?

I was born in the countryside near the French Alps. A stunning part of the world. I used to go skiing a lot when I was a kid, the mountains were just there. But my favourite was spring and summer with all the flowers in bloom. I went back for the first time in many years, two summers ago with my dad and the landscapes were even more stunning and breath-taking than I remembered. The air is extremely sharp and pure due to the altitude. It kind of burns your nostrils and lungs!

OK, I shall stop here for now. I will write more later on.

Sunday 14th March

9.15am Sunday now, full sunshine. Outside my window, there is a plum tree which is currently in full bloom, covered in white flowers and if I open the window, it smells of honey as if there is a giant pot of honey in my garden! Priceless.

The most amazing info for me in your letter is that you got married to a pen friend and are now divorcing. You have to tell me more about that. This must be a special relationship you have with this woman for sure. How are you feeling about this experience?

How many pen friends have you got now? It would be nice for you to have someone from every continent. :-)

You mention the guards. How are they? Friendly or not? Your vision of people living like lemmings made me smile. I am going to let you discover for yourself why I said I am original and a bit of an artist. And it seems that you are too!

I don't think that our personalities will clash but I can imagine that we will have our ups and downs. That is the nature of human connections: complex and simple at the same time.

It is one week now that I have not been able to go for a walk. I am stuck inside the house and it brings waves of anger and even rage. Yesterday I ended up shaking my body for quite some time and then doing some yoga and stretches. I felt more at peace afterwards.

What are your strategies to cope with stress and strong emotions?

I love your smiley faces. Hey, you don't and can't bore me! I feel that there is so much you can give me, teach me, show me. And vice versa. :-)

Evening now: I have had a bit of a rough day to be honest, challenged physically, challenged emotionally. This evening it is quite cold outside, so the giant pot of honey is not smelling. My friend Lisa came to visit me today and she cooked handmade pizzas for us and we had a lovely time together. She is a gentle woman. It was really nice.

I have a few more questions for you: Can you do sport? Who comes to visit you? Do you have to work? Do you have friends inside "this place"?

It is going to be quite a process to get to know each other! It is actually unusual to write letters nowadays when everybody emails or is on their mobile phone. I think you say cell phone in the US. I love writing. After my sister died over six years ago, I was extremely distressed, and I started to write a letter to her. I wrote roughly for two years. When I stopped I named this piece of writing: "The

Mystical Journey of a Letter". I have self-published it on Amazon. At the moment I am writing a book on the spiritual processes of life and death. Do you keep a journal or write for yourself?

My mum who is 85 is not too good. She is usually strong and funny. She is Scottish. My dad is arriving on Monday to look after me as my operation is on Thursday. It's going to be special to have him around. He is 83 and still in top form. He was pretty absent as a dad when I was growing up so it is going to be quite a unique experience for me and Scarlet to have him look after us.

A bit about my evening rituals: I am now going to do some yogic breathing. Breathe with awareness. It gives me lots of energy and is calming. Plus, it soothes pain. Then I shall listen to some relaxing music which balances the brain and helps with pain. I will set an intention for my sleep and relax my body deeply. So much about being original **:-)**! Do you have rituals in your day?

Scarlet is watching a DVD in her bedroom. I will brush my teeth and then off I go.

Un pokito Espanol para la noche: bone noche, las estrellas en el ciela e la luna…

Bonne nuit in French.

Tuesday: It is now my turn to feel anxious that my letter is a bore. Remember, this is my first time writing to an "inmate".

When I receive your next letter, I shall be recovering and on my way to health again. Houra!

My dad is going to the post office for me. I am going to tell him now who I am writing to. He does not know yet.

I am really looking forward to discovering more about your life in "that place".

Best wishes,
Suzanne

March 28th, 2015

> March 28, 2015
>
> Hello Suzanne,
>
> How are you feeling? I hope my letter finds you feeling better in your recovery and that my letter brings a smile to you. I received your letter and it was great to hear from you and thank you for the violet flower. I was pleasantly surprised to get it and it brought some color to this dreary place.

Well, mi amiga, you do ask a lot of questions and I want to respond to your letter page by page, so I know I won't miss anything. :-)

Today is a Saturday and I have come in from recreation pens. This is quite an event here. It is one of the times when we have to be stripped searched. After we have our hands handcuffed behind us we line up in a red square until all who are going out are there. Then we walk to the 10 feet by 10 feet steel cages where we each go inside one. There are 10. This is the only place we can talk face to face with each other. We never have physical contact with anyone except when we are handcuffed.

Anyway, it was a nice morning and I was able to take bread out so I could feed those little birds that are all around. Now, I am back in my cell after I showered. I put ear plugs in so I can just concentrate on writing. This is a way to escape for a while.

I don't want to overload you with letters. I don't want you to think I'm weird :-). I'm joking. I am grateful you chose to write to me. I know people on the row tend to get a bad name. Thank you for seeing me as a person and not as a killer. I know that you do not know the whole story as to why I am here but I was obviously convicted of murder as this is the only crime in America that carries a death sentence.

I do try to meditate at least every day, sometimes it is hard. I have a special place in my mind that I go to. It often varies depending on my mood. But my process is to put ear plugs in, usually after the guards do their hourly walk. I sit on a folded blanket on the floor, no specific position, just so I am comfortable. I close my eyes, slow my breathing and relax letting my mind drift.

My meditation spot changes but my most frequent area I go to in my mind is a place in Idaho called The Shoshone Falls. There is a little platform there and if you stand at the edge you can feel the mist of the falls. It is so peaceful there. I tend to turn my fan on low so there is a cool breeze, there I can release tension or stress. I am in my special place for thirty to forty-five minutes. I get up regenerated.

What we call "death row", I usually just say "this place" or "the row". There is really not a set name. It just depends on what we are talking about.

I had to smile :-) as I read about the mountains in the French Alps. It had to have an amazing view and the air had to be refreshing to your lungs. I felt a little envious. :-)

As for the guards, every day varies. They usually treat us with respect but there are a few who try to get a negative reaction. Some guards come in with an attitude or they simply have a bad day. They will often nit-pick on some of the rules or they'll be sarcastic and try to get a person to yell back at them. I don't talk to them. It just prevents any conflict.

To deal with stress or strong emotions, I meditate every day and it helps a lot. If I get really frustrated, I will do an intense workout in my cell, but that hasn't happened for a while. I do get depressed sometimes.

When I am depressed or if I get too stressed, I tell the guys that I need to escape for a few days. I go to the front of my cell and tell a few people I talk to mostly that I am going to disappear for a few days. If someone did not hear that I am escaping and does call me, the guys I told, will let him know I am taking a break. Out of respect for them, they know I can't answer because I need some time to myself.

This means I don't talk to anyone. I put earplugs in or listen to music. I close in on myself to deal with the depression or stress. I sometimes will write everything on paper and send it to my friend in Switzerland. When she gets it she burns it to release those feelings. It takes about a week to get to her. I can tell because about six to eight days later, I feel a release and I am lighter. I don't know if it's just in my mind, but it helps.

If I get angry with someone in here or have an issue, I just don't talk to them. This can sometimes be comical. One time I had an argument with a guy in a cell upstairs. I don't remember over what, but it was over something small as most arguments here are. He would stand at the front of his cell and yell down at me. But I didn't want to argue so I put my headphones on and listened to my radio. The volume was up so I didn't hear him. My neighbour told me later that he kept arguing for 20 minutes before he realised, I had left the argument.

I don't get any visits. All or most of my family lives far away in another state. I occasionally get a visit from my lawyer. But I have a tendency to not talk much, except as you can see in letters.

Another of my flaws, I guess you can call it that, is that I don't get close to men. Throughout my life when I had a best friend it was a girl or a woman. I just click better. That is another story for another letter. I do have a few guys I consider friends but as you get to know me you'll see that the words "Friend" and "Friendship" are precious to me. I treasure those words and they mean a lot to me.

Alright now, my turn for a few questions:

When you look into a mirror what do you see?

Besides your daughter what do you consider is most important to you?

During your day what is the one ritual besides meditation you do or must do?

When you meditate do you have an inner place you go to?

For me, my sanity is most important. I know this is vague but in here you can lose your sanity quickly, so I always need to stay busy to keep my mind moving and thinking on what I am doing.

The one ritual I must do is drink my coffee when I get up. During this time, I decide what I will do for the day. I never have a fixed schedule because we don't know if they will change recreation or do cell searches. So I try to keep it flexible but I do make a plan for the day. I don't always stick to it but I try to stay as close as I can.

About the mirror question, I'll wait for your answer because there is a specific reason I asked it.

Smile it is good for you. Robert

Tuesday, 8th April 2015

Hi Robert,

It is nearly three weeks after the operation. It feels much longer! A pretty flat Suzanne is writing to you today. But I want to write as a means to escape my self-pity and total self-centredness and to say hello.

I knew it was going to be tough after the operation, but it has been super tough! I have experienced physical pain like never before which was psychologically traumatic. I had an allergic reaction to the morphine, so I was left with just normal pain killers which were not strong enough. The pain drained my spirit. That was the first week. Since then it has been a journey of re-learning to move my body, being able to stand straight and slowly walking again.

The good news is that they saved my uterus but a by-product has been that my guts have shifted and this is extremely painful too.

OK, enough on my lows but I have to say that it is actually good that we can do this with each other: show our unhappy self and not just our happy one. You can write to me anytime you are low too.

Guess what? I am also a fan of Ayla and Jondalar of the Children of the Earth. I am on book seven. I am reading it in French though. I love it and I really believe that they are important books for us to remember about mankind's journey. We have lost so much wisdom since the times of Ayla and Jondalar 35,000 years ago. It is amazing we both love those books. I laughed in fact when I read about your taste of books and films: we are well matched indeed!

I have had many paranormal experiences myself since being a child although I don't call them like that but multidimensional experiences. I can share some with you if you want. Have you had any? I believe in UFOs and aliens. We cannot be the only planet with life and intelligence in the entire universe. I regard animals, plants and cells as extremely intelligent. But we humans have not quite mastered our brains and minds yet, hence the state of the world!

I want to thank you for sharing more about your life and how you ended up where you are. From the beginning I had decided that I would treat you with respect and see your life as this sacred, unique journey with its karma that you have created for your soul and spirit to evolve.

This is a powerful karmic incarnation you are in, in this lifetime. Please tell me what you think about that. Some of my views are Buddhist in essence but now, in the last six years, I have gone deeper into soul, spirit and multi-dimensional awareness.

I know it is easy to play the victim of our circumstances. Let me tell you, I have acted as Queen Victim for over two decades of my adult life until I realised that it was not helping me. My ultimate quest nowadays is to maintain inner freedom and peace in any given moment. Well, that is a quest I have not enjoyed since the operation. :-)

I am sad that the death penalty still exists in the world. Maybe I am naive? Idealistic yes! But hey, it is through visions that we change the world for the better. I have faith in our evolution and our capacity to harmonise with each other, life, the planet and consciousness.

In the last few days, I have felt pretty lonely. My dad left one week ago. How do you cope with loneliness?

OK, I will stop here for today. I really enjoyed connecting with you on paper. Take care.

P.S. Can you hug your fellow inmates or some of the guards? Suzanne X :-)

April 4th 2015

Hello Suzanne,

How are you doing? I hope my letter finds you doing better and healing fast. I am doing well, just trying to stay busy and out of trouble. :-)

Well today is the first day of a week-long journal, so you can get an idea of what a typical day for me is like. Though my days often vary, the basic routine stays the same. I wasn't sure how I wanted to do this diary, but I have decided to just write at the end of every day. Let's see how that works out. I have a cheap $9 Casio watch. Although it's cheap, it's durable. And it keeps me up to date with the time.

Monday. Alright, Monday is a recreation day, so I went out into the small pens to walk around and just talk. It is getting warmer out so it means more people will start to go out. My typical routine for a recreation day is to get our breakfast and lunch sacks at about 5am. I'll eat my cookie and cereal, take one piece of bread out to take with me for the pens. I like to feed the birds. By the way, I never eat fresh food like fruit or vegetables.

At about 6.30am the guards start pulling us to go out. We are out for two hours and a half. Then I come in to shower. I go back to my cell, put my toiletries on the ledge and hang my laundry. Oh yeah, I tend to do my own white laundry (boxers, sheets, pillowcase and socks) in the shower. So I wash them at shower time.

When I go to the shower, I grab my shower stuff (towel, soap, shampoo, extra boxer shorts, clean t-shirts, washcloth) and put them in the laundry bag. The guard comes to my cell front. Sometimes, but rarely they'll inspect the items to make sure I'm not passing stuff by leaving it in the shower. I am handcuffed, taken to the shower, once the door is shut the handcuffs are taken off, the guard leaves and I shower. Usually I am there for 45 minutes to an hour. The guard comes back, handcuffs on again, takes me back to my cell and leaves. I have gotten to the point that I now just bird bath or often wash myself completely in my cell at my sink and mop up the water with a towel. It is easier and takes 20 minutes in total.

When everything is put away, I get my blanket, ear plugs and put it in a certain spot. I turn my fan on low so I feel the breeze and I close my eyes and meditate to get out of here.

Around 11.30am to 12pm, I do a little thirty minutes exercise. This is new so I am still getting used to it. I don't want to sweat too much. Whenever I am done and cooled down, I take a quick bird bath, basically just wipe myself down with a washcloth.

I then get my radio and sit on my bed to relax. I typically listen to 70s, 80s, 90s and Spanish music and some of the newer stuff. I like slow jams. I do this until 2pm. Then I turn my TV on and watch TV shows. At 3pm I watch People Court and then at 4pm Caso's Cerrados. They are reality TV court shows where one person can sue another in front of an arbitrator that is the judge or decision maker. Both sides sign a binding contract that whatever the arbitrator decides, will be the ruling.

I like this because it has interesting cases and the judge is into learning about the lives of both plaintiffs and defendants. There seems to be fairness for both sides.

At 4.30pm, I write letters if I have any to write. Lately there haven't been many. The rest of the day I channel surf. Today is World Wrestling Entertainment at 5pm, so I will watch that for three hours.

At 8pm, I get things ready for the next day. At 9pm, I watch a soap opera on Telemundo which is an American channel in Spanish. At 10pm, I typically get ready for bed. For this week, I will do this at 10.30pm as I will be writing to you. Oh, I forgot when I get back from the shower, I prepare a cup of coffee. Good to have that coffee.

This is a typical routine on recreation days which is usually on a Monday, Wednesday and Friday. The weekend is different, but I will write about it then. Nothing really happens on Mondays.

Tuesday. Alright, a new day, a bit busy. My days on Tuesday and Thursday are lazy days. At 5am we must get our breakfast and lunch. I usually eat the cereal bar and cookie. Then I go back to sleep and usually roll out of bed at 9 or 10am again. I drink my coffee and prepare for the day. I do my usual meditation. I don't skip this much because it is one of the few things that keeps me sane. The only difference from a recreation day and the other days is sleeping in. Otherwise it is a mirror image of my weekdays.

Today is inmate store day so at about 3pm they bring our orders. This week was a treat because the store had an overflow of old Christmas treats, primarily, Kellog's Red Velvet pop tarts. They are so delicious, and it was a treat I almost never get. I don't order a lot of food anymore, but I did some work and got paid so I spoiled myself.

I usually stay up a little later because the graveyard shift (this is the guards' third shift from 10pm to 6am) passes out the sheets for us to order for next week.

Other than that, it was a typical day so let me close here for now.

Wednesday. Today is typically a busy day. Property and secure packs get passed out. Secure packs are linked to a website that people on our phone or visiting list can go to, to order us groceries. Orange laundry (shorts, t-shirts, sweats, pants) get handed in. It is also a recreation day and today I went out, but I stayed to myself in my cage. I typically talk to someone, but some guys were arguing, and it just takes too much energy to talk over them. So, I sat in a corner and watched the birds come get my bread.

I was a bit irritated when I came in, so I decided to work out before I showered. I got in there at 10.48 am, did what I had to. Got back to the cell. We never leave or come back to our cell without a guard escorting us and being handcuffed. Afterwards, I just got my walkman and stayed sitting on the spot listening to the radio. I kind of regretted it because at 1.47pm I got up to get ready for TV and my butt hurt!

During TV, I filled out my store sheet. Ordered my typical stuff like toiletries, phone time, writing material, stamps and coffee. If there is extra money, I'll buy mixed nuts, tortillas and refried beans.

Oh, today is library day too. Let me explain. On Sundays, I put in an order for five books and stick it out of my front door so the guards can pick it up. On Wednesdays, the books come and are usually passed out when we get our laundry back. We can keep books for two weeks, but we can order one every week.

Dinner today was at 5pm. The kitchen sends two refrigerator type carts (one hot, one cold). They have the food trays for all 60 cells in the cluster. As the guard goes from pod to pod, they stack 10 cold trays and 10 hot trays on a small serving cart. Each tray is protected by a lid. They open the food traps, remove the lid and give us the trays. We eat and about 45 minutes later they come back to pick up the trays.

The food trap is hard to explain, it is about halfway down the door of the cell. It is five and a half inches wide and 18 inches long. On the outside it has a lock on it that the guards have to unlock whenever they give us something. It is otherwise always shut. We also put our hands out through the trap when we are handcuffed behind our backs.

After dinner I sat back and read for a few hours. I checked out "light a distant fire" by Lucia St Clair Robson. It's a book about an Indian tribe in Florida. It is OK. I think it's a love story.

Rest of the day was the novella, a soap opera in Spanish on the Telemundo Channel. Then to bed.

Thursday. Today was more than a lazy day. White laundry gets handed in. No recreation so I didn't roll out of bed until a little after 11 am. I drank my coffee and did my meditation. Afterwards, I didn't work out, instead I put music on and walked for two hours. Unfortunately, we aren't allowed batteries, so we need electricity for the Walkman. When I walk around my cell, I put it on the table and let its cord hang down and I walk around my cell in a figure of eight from one corner to the next. To not pull it off the table, I switch the cord from one hand to the other.

Then I watched my programs. At 5.30pm I started to read a little but didn't get far. Started talking to my neighbours. We talk cell to cell, but I can't see them. If it is a long conversation, I go to the front of the cell and sit on the toilet so I can hear better. We ended up talking until past 9pm. My neighbour can talk! The only thing that saved me was my novella, my beloved soap opera in Spanish. After the novella I laid down and did some deep breathing. I put on the fan and my eye covers and just slowly inhaled and exhaled until I fell asleep. It is now technically Friday because it is 4.19am but I wanted to write for Thursday. See today was a lazy day.

Friday. I just read what I wrote earlier. Oh, boy, was I lazy. Today wasn't really any different. I got up only because it is recreation day. It's for level three guys and I am at level three. This is how the prison keeps track of what privileges each individual inmate is allowed. A level three is the highest level and so we get three phone calls a week (15 minutes each), recreation in the small pens four times a week and go out to the tables with another person. The guards put on a belly chain which is a chain that goes around our waist with a handcuff on each side of our body. We get taken to a table at the front of the pod. We sit down. A chain is connected to the chair and hooked onto the belly chain. One hand is handcuffed to the table and the other is let free. We sit there for two hours playing games like connect four, dominoes or chess.

At level three, we are allowed to buy up to $100 worth from the store a week (well, if you have that kind of money that is!). Level one is the lowest and has a lot less privileges. You lose your electricity. Losing privileges happens when you get into trouble. A guard writes a disciplinary ticket. Then, you see a hearing officer. If you lose privileges it is for 15 to 30 days. To gain them back you have to go to classes. It takes six months to a year to get raised back to level three. After your 15 or 30 days are up, you get your electricity back and can purchase food items from the store.

In total, I have received three disciplinary tickets since being on the row. All for disobeying staff and fighting. My last ticket was in 2000 for fighting on the chain gang.

Today, they didn't take us out until 2.30pm, too late for me so I ended up meditating early and exercising. I didn't go for a regular shower and I washed myself in my cell. This is a pain because I have to clean up all the water on the floor, then do laundry in the sink. I got done at 10am give or take a few minutes. I finished reading the library book. So, by 1pm I was ready for music.

The rest of the day was boring. I am now just waiting for the guard to bring our weekly issue of one roll of toilet paper and then I'll go to sleep. It sounds like he's a few pods away.

Saturday. Well, today was phone call day. I typically call my mum every six days and my friend in Switzerland every twelve days. The days vary depending on when it's our pod's day for the phone. We are supposed to get it every odd day of the month, but there are three pods with odd numbers and there are only two phones. I can only call on two different days as long as I don't call three times on one day. Does that make sense?

Anyway, a routine Saturday is to get up for recreation at 6 am. Today we went out at about 7am. I came in after 9.30am and took a shower. Back in my cell by 10.15am, put the shower stuff up, hung laundry to dry and got ready to meditate. At 10.28am I was sitting, relaxing and disappearing from here for a while. I got the phone after

11am and called my mom and then my friend. After that, I waited, so the guard could move the phone. Then I took a nap for three hours.

There are two ways to make phone calls. We can call collect, for this the person has to put money on an account with the phone company. Or we can purchase phone time through the inmate store. In order to call internationally it is $7 for 15 minutes. It is less than $4 to phone my mum.

Calling my mum was hard at first, because of all that I have put her through, but now I have to call her every six days, so I know she is good and to hear her voice.

At about 4pm after I washed my face, I watched a little bit of TV and at 6pm I worked out. It was more to tire me out. Then I took a bird bath and sat back, listened to some music for the rest of the evening. While I am listening to music, I draw or fill in puzzles. Then at about 10.30pm, I will lay down and breathe consciously for a while until I fall asleep.

It was not a real productive or busy day, but most weekends aren't. Saturdays are typically the most boring day during the week.

Sunday. It's 7.30pm and I want to write about today so I can get this in the envelope and on its way. I have to leave my outgoing mail on my door by 10pm. We can send mail out Sunday night to Thursday night. The rest of the nights the guards don't pick it up.

Today is a lazy day. I typically sleep in as long as I can on Sundays. Today I got up at 11.30am. I washed my face and got ready to meditate which I did at 12pm. I tried to stay away for as long as I could and was able to mediate for close to an hour.

At about 1.30pm I started to watch TV and sat down to put my book request form together for library this week. Remember? I needed to write for a clothing exchange and then I finished some letters.

I will watch TV for the rest of the evening. If nothing is on, I'll listen to music on the radio. Sometimes I stay up all night because everyone is asleep, so it's quiet and I can concentrate more on my meditation. When it is quiet like that I feel more at ease and more relaxed. When it's like this I don't have to put earplugs in to block the noise, so I can really relax.

At about 10pm this evening, I'll lay back and put my headphones on and listen to music for two hours and at midnight I'll get up and see what is on TV. I have to get up at 5am to collect breakfast/lunch tomorrow and this will be the start of a new week.

This was a typical week. It only changes if I get some work to do from other inmates. Then I spend most of the week doing that. It's not all that interesting and it is easy to just be lazy but in here, if you don't keep your mind moving it is really easy to lose your mind, so I have to always be doing something. That's why I like writing letters.

Anyway, my friend, that's it for this letter. I hope you are well and healing quickly. I hope to hear from you soon so until then please take care of yourself and be safe.

Robert

Sunday 11th April 2015

Dear Robert,

I wrote to you on Tuesday and on Wednesday I received a letter from you. Thanks. It is the longest read I have had since the operation. I have read it twice already and I am embarking on another read to reply to it. :-)

Your questions have triggered me. I love them.

A little setting first: it is 10am, after a week of gorgeous spring sunny weather, it is now grey sky and raining. I actually love it, it is soothing and calming. I am on my own with Couscous, our cat, as Scarlet stayed overnight at her boyfriend's!

The last few days have been tough with pain. My uterus is going through a revolution. I am back on full number of painkillers but still after two to three hours their effect wears off. Last night, I thought that I might need to go to hospital as the pain grew aggressive. I have decided to shift my response to it which was fear based and I am learning to relax into it. So, I did lots of breathing, super gentle massage of my belly with lavender essential oil, which is calming and repeating "I surrender". My night ended up not too bad. I was meditating at 4am and apart from a few crises I managed to sleep.

I love getting to know you. I think of you frequently and about the complexities of your life. The rhythm of our letters is painfully slow yet grounding as to touch paper and witness handwritten words holds a deeper weight than those typed for a screen. The world at large has lost the art of letter writing, "letter posting" and "letter reading". But we two are still sharing that gift of slow pace. I am growing to like it!

Thank you for your description of your outing process at the recreation pens. This was quite difficult to read. It feels inhuman and extreme from my perspective. But as I took it in, I relaxed into being able to discover your life as neutrally as possible. In due course I would also love to learn about your fellow inmates.

I love your act of giving bread to the birds. I do little things like that myself. I adore birds. At the end of my meditation at 5am this morning, all the birds were singing, and it felt like the most beautiful concerto in the world. Humans have not invented music, birds have!

The lemmings made me smile because I could sense your sharp observation. I like that. You are very wise about not getting involved in arguments. I have come to the same conclusion. As for writing down your negativity and then having your Swiss sister burn it for you, I totally believe in this kind of energy work so it makes total sense for me that you would feel the release of it being burnt even at a distance. I have had many experiences of distant healing and know that at the level of energy there is no space and no separation. I am happy that you do this when needed. :-)

Concrete questions for you now: what is the role of your lawyer? What can he/she do for you? I understand you have been on the row for eighteen years now. Why so long? What is next? What is your relationship to the future? Not easy questions to ask but you have said that it's OK for me to be radical!

And I have some more for you in fact: Have you made peace with your past? How does it feel to know that you have killed? How do you feel about your punishment from society?

Well, yours was a fantastic question: what do I see when I look in the mirror? Makes me think that maybe you do not have access to seeing your own face. Do you? OK, let me move in front of a mirror.

I expect the answer would be different depending on my mood but today I see a woman who is starting to age, has wrinkles, grey hair (I have decided not to dye my hair anymore). I look both extremely drained (from the operation) and rested. I see someone who is calm and aspires to inner peace. I see a free spirit inside a body. I see how difficult it is to fully love and embrace myself simply for who I am. Normally, I wear quite a lot of jewellery but not since the operation.

I see what I don't like about myself. I struggle with the ageing part! I see a human being who desires compassion and unconditional love. I mostly see tiredness this morning to be fair. I have green eyes and I love their colour. Usually, they are strong and sparkly but this morning they look like they need support and sleep.

I am going to stop here for now and indeed go for a rest. More later today... Ciao...

1.30pm, I have slept a bit, eaten, now I am drinking a super weak coffee, I call it my homeopathic coffee, and this is how I like it. It shifts energy that way.

Onto your next question: the most important thing besides my daughter? I have to say my health: physical, mental and emotional. I have spent years dealing with health issues and could not be properly a mum to Scarlet so I know this is vital. When bereaved I lost my emotional balance which then impacted negatively on my physical fitness. I can 100% relate to your answer about remaining sane. I imagine you have become an expert at that!

I love your rituals question: In the evenings and sometimes during the night when I can't sleep, I open my bedroom window to breathe in the fresh air. Even in full winter, when it is freezing outside, I quickly open the window. I love breathing the fresh (urban!) air, feeling its temperature and humidity on my skin. Sometimes I see the stars and the moon or the typical London ceiling of low clouds with its light pollution colours. It is my ritual to remember that I belong to the universe, to connect again and again with the extraordinary dimensions of life and that I am but a tiny speck in this universe. It calms me, it soothes me, it helps me let go of issues. My problems become nothing when viewed from the perspective of stars and infinity. I feel alive and that, in itself, is a gift. Sometimes I even call Scarlet in this ritual when something special catches my eyes, nostrils or ears. We love sharing this magical moment together.

Do you have a window in your cell? When do you see the sky?

It is now Sunday 10am. I got really tired and drained yesterday and could not write anymore. I am controlling the pain with regular massages with lavender essential oil. I still have regular sharp pain but otherwise it is much better.

Now onto your important question about meditation. I am so happy you are a meditation buddy. :-) Over the last five years meditating has become an increasingly important part of my life. I practice different types of meditation. Let me explain. I do one type called the Endorphin Effect and this is exactly what you do when you go into your special feel-good place in Idaho. Those feel-good meditations, generate endorphins in the body which are our natural, healing morphine type hormones! I know all that because I did a weekend long course on that subject.

I have two special places I go to: the Alps and the sea near my mum's. In the Alps, I always go to the same valley which is one of the most stunning places I have ever been to. My other spot is a ten-minute drive from my mum's flat in South Brittany, in France. There is an inland sea, its shores are wild forests. It is incredibly beautiful. I also think of the people I love, my cat, scents – mostly roses (hence I have smeared some solid rose perfume on this page), in short anything to promote feeling good so those hormones get activated.

The other type of meditation I do is heart based. I bring my breathing, focus and awareness into my heart area (or heart chakra. Do you know about chakras?) and I generate feelings of peaceful love and joyous compassion. I often lay my hands on my heart during this process. If I feel angry, I feel love and compassion for my anger, if I feel sad, I feel love and compassion for my sadness. It is powerful.

Another type of meditation I do stills my thinking and my breathing. I bring my awareness into nothingness (which is bliss) and I linger there feeling the eternity of the present moment. Those moments are healing and transformative as when I go back into my daily life, I am a new Suzanne!

On a regular basis I attend three to five days workshops where we meditate like that with around five hundred people and I learn about applied neuroscience and quantum physics, and epigenetics. I will tell you more about that for sure. I have had multidimensional experiences at those times. This summer, I will attend another workshop in Germany. I can't wait. They are also tough and intense because we push ourselves outside our comfort zone on many levels and we meditate for about seven hours per day and the rest of the day we study intensively.

I love your description of your coffee ritual.

I believe in existence after death. I saw and felt my sister's spirit at the exact time of her dying although I had no idea that she was dying. There were beings of light with her. It is the most powerful and extremely beautiful event I have encountered. It has changed my destiny. I am not afraid to say this.

I am going to stop as I am already feeling quite drained but need to go for a little walk, walking is a key to my recovery.

Angeles para tu!
Suzanne

PS. Thanks for making me laugh with your joke of you not wanting me to think that you are weird, plus, I love your drawing of the smiley face. It helps.

April 21st 2015

Hello Suzanne,

How has everything been? I hope you are feeling better. I am doing good. Just trying to stay busy and out of trouble. I received your letter with the perfume. I transferred it to a piece of paper and put it in my vent so most of my cell smells of it. :-)

A quick setting, I am sitting on my bed with the TV on, which is normal since it's on from the time I get out of bed until I go to bed. I like the constant movement.

Right now, there are only two of us in the pod. A pod consists of 10 cells, two showers and one recreation pen which is walled up with concrete and a metal grate at the top so the sun can shine in. The rest went to class. I drew the short end of the stick so was left out this time. I'll probably end up going with people from other pods. It was pretty quiet while I read your letter and that is always great.

Real quick, about the class. A while back, a lawsuit was filed against the prison about the conditions in our unit and other maximum-security prisons. A settlement was made. We would be allowed to get out of our cells for nine and half hours a week and have better contact with other inmates. So, we were given the 10 recreations pens side by side. Before them, we were allowed to go into a single recreation pen which is at the end of the pod, it is bigger, but you are alone.

We were expecting a few other things that haven't happened yet and we were told that in order to get the new privileges we had to take classes designated by the administration. Then that changed from being mandatory to voluntary. I always want to go and attend because I can communicate with other people without a cage in between. But this is a different letter topic.

I'd like to hear about your paranormal experiences. I have had a few. One of them was when I was 10 years old. My mom was going to see my grandma and I didn't want to go so I was going to stay with an aunt. But I kept getting a feeling that I should go, so I went. I got my two cousins to come, so my aunt decided to join too. When we got back hours later, the apartment had been on fire. I think that maybe if I hadn't gotten that feeling then it is possible, they would have been hurt in the fire. It is small stuff like that.

As for UFOs and aliens, I believe they exist, and I think that in the near future they'll pay us a public visit. I am reminded of the lines in the film "Contact" where she is asked by a kid if she believes in aliens and she says that if they don't exist "it is a pretty big waste of space".

As for the state of the world, I think that we are young in terms of evolution and that the real important question is: will we grow into our better selves before we hit a no going back situation when it comes to the abuses we lay upon mother earth? I mean, will we evolve enough to realise that we must protect our planet and make sure we don't abuse what we have but respect it. Will we learn that by continuing to wage wars or being filled with ideological hate we are in fact only destroying the precious resources we have?

Wars and hate are only bringing negative energy and eventually the earth will be done with us. I think that she is trying to purge herself of us and of our abuses by bigger tornadoes, hurricanes, droughts, tsunamis, typhoons and other weather phenomena. In doing so, many lives are lost. I just hope we learn before it's too late.

I regret the choices I have made and if given the opportunity I would do it differently, but the world doesn't work that way. I know a lot of people see the crime and not the person. Truth be told if you knew me one year before I was arrested, you would have thought I could never do what I did. But in life, we are faced with choices and decisions. We can take different roads, some bumpier than others. I unfortunately made the wrong decision and people were hurt; families destroyed as well as my own life. All I can do is better myself so when the time comes, I am prepared for my next incarnation and make a positive difference there. Does that make sense?

I think that my situation on the row is one in which I am meant to gain knowledge for myself and others.

You asked what I do to cope with being lonely. A difficult question to answer. It is hard to deal with loneliness here because we deal with it so much. I am kind of more adapted to it I guess then most others because growing up I was quiet and a loner. I didn't trust a lot of people. What I mean by this is that I have days when I would rather be by myself, so I don't have to talk or deal with the drama in here. Other days I will talk to someone about small stuff just to hear a voice. But the truly hard loneliness is physical. I don't mean sexual, but even just to be able to shake someone's hand, to feel a warm hug. To be deprived from any slightest bit of physical contact: that is the true loneliness. I am only touched when handcuffed.

Our sexual desire is something that we must take care of ourselves. Before, we were allowed pornographic magazines so we could look at naked women and masturbate. Now we use our imagination. Often, I'll be reading a book and if there is an explicit scene, I imagine it is me and masturbate. It is unfortunate that we must experience our sexual desires like this. If we gain more freedom in the future, I am sure some men will share their bodies with other guys but for me I love women so I will just continue to relieve myself. Unfortunately, because the prison has become stricter even explicit books are prevented from being sent by the outside world.

I want to say thank you for finding me. You truly honour me, and I can say that I also am glad that we were matched up together and I do cherish our friendship. I believe that we'll learn a lot from each other and that we'll become great friends. As for the complexities of my life and situation, know that your letters do help to cope with it all. For those few hours that I receive your letter and write back, I am able to escape this place.

I am able to disappear. I put earplugs in and concentrate. For those moments I am not here, I am in a park writing. Receiving your letters is like receiving a gift from the outside because I get to share your experiences. I get to be there when you are writing. It is a relief to be able to concentrate on your stories and what you share.

I love your description of bird singing and it being the best music in the world. It is amazing how much those little things can bring a smile to my face. It is one of the reasons I like to feed them. Once one came down and ate a little, it chirped and sang as if to tell his friends that dinner is served or rather breakfast. I joke with one of the guys that I bring the appetizer since I bring only one slice of bread. He brings six to eight slices. I am just warming them up.

The noise heard from my cell can sometimes feel overwhelming: people flushing their toilets, having conversations about television programs or politics. They are usually respectful chats and often the guys don't talk over each other, but it is loud and constant enough that if I try to meditate I can still hear them. I prefer silence and the best way to obtain it is to put earplugs in. The guards often don't like it because they end up banging on the cell front to get my attention as I can't hear them either.

The guards come into the pod every hour to do their hourly count and make sure everyone is doing what they are meant to do. They look into each cell through the cell front which is a bunch of small holes about one centimetre in diameter.

If they need something, have cleaning supplies or food trays and I have my earplugs in, they will bang until I respond. If I am laying down and not moving, they also call out to see me move. They are not allowed to enter our cells unless we are handcuffed except when there is an emergency or when they come in, in force to record everything with a handheld camera.

About being a meditation buddy, yep I am one. For me meditating is the most vital routine I have. If I don't do it, I am crabby and short tempered. It helps me to relax but it also rejuvenates me, I have more energy and feel like physically moving around more. I can then deal with this place.

It is amazing to see how grown men can become little children. They argue over small stuff like if one person has an opinion or believes to be correct and the other disagrees, it can turn into an argument. It becomes childish and sometimes leads to name calling. I am sure I have done this too but since I started to seriously meditate, I have gained renewed strength. By renewed strength I mean that I am more aware and tolerant of the childish arguments and I am more apt to avoid them.

The building I am in, is in a maximum-security unit. There are 12 clusters. A cluster is an area in the prison, that's what we call it and in each cluster, there are six pods. The clusters are divided into four wings. Death row is on wing three. There are only two clusters of pods for death row which make 120 cells. We wear orange clothing except boxers, socks and shoes, those are white. If we leave the cluster, we must wear orange pants and t-shirts. It used to be a jumpsuit, but they have moved towards pants.

Alright, I want to reply to your response to my question about what you see when you look in the mirror. I asked this for two reasons. One, you can get an insight into someone on how they respond, secondly when I started to grow and evolve about eight to nine years of being here, it was because of a poem I read about looking at oneself in a mirror.

I love your response. I see that you are a genuine person (I knew that already) and that despite a few qualms with yourself, you accept who you are. Thank you for being so open.

My turn, what do I see in the mirror? I see a balding, ageing man with a moustache and soul patch who needs to lose some weight. That's the outside. Inside, I see a man who has struggled to become better than he was in the past. One who knows that only he can truly enact the proper change in himself. I see someone who still fights demons from his past but one who does it in a more productive and peaceful way than he used to. I see a guy who wants to continue to gain knowledge and peace.

Until next time, smile. Robert

Wednesday 22nd April 2015

Hi Buddy,

I knew this morning that I was going to write to you today and I also felt that I was going to receive a letter from you. And I did!:-)

I want to first acknowledge your "get well soon" card. It is amazing. It is on my chest of drawers. Scarlet is very impressed by your art and bubble writing as she calls it. Then there is also your card for her birthday. I have not told her, of course. It is so balanced, proportioned and beautiful. Don't be offended but do you copy your drawings, or do they come from your mind? :-)

We did say honesty, yes!? So, here is honesty: your last letter, your week's long journal, it did upset me. The reality of your daily life hit me. Thank you for keeping this journal. A real eye opener. I want to apologise for the stupid questions I have asked you in previous letters like: can you wear what you want? I feel stupid now. But that is OK. I am OK feeling ignorant and stupid.

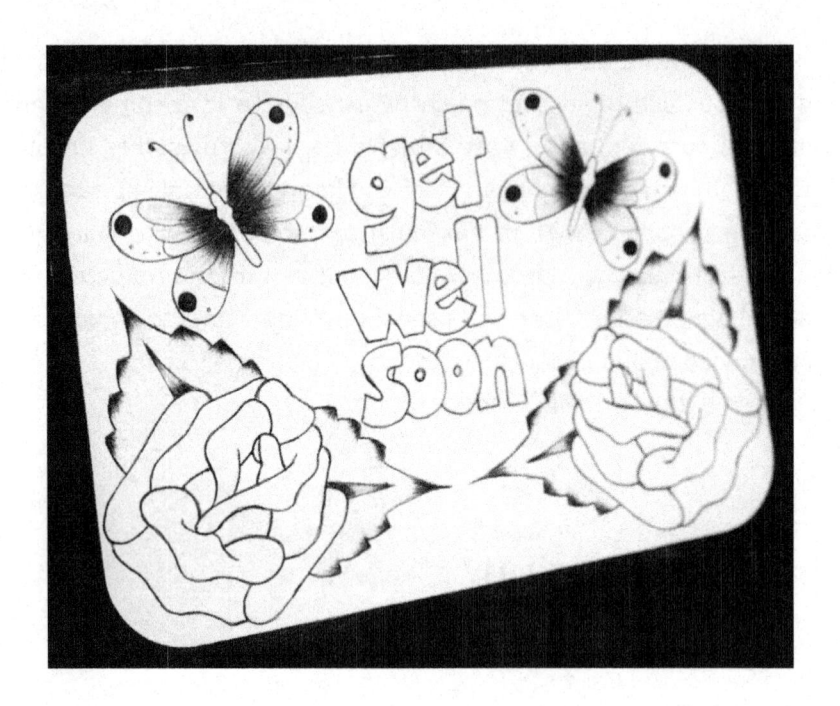

I really enjoyed your sketches of the cells, pods. It is useful to get a concrete idea of the layout of your environment. Scarlet read your journal. She has expressed a great interest about you and has now followed a BBC TV series of documentaries on death row.

Will you send your daughter a card for her birthday?

I am really excited about a few things in my life at the moment and really want to share those with you. I came across for the third time now, a traditional Hawaiian prayer called Ho'oponopono. It is simple and extremely profound when practiced. It is based on the principles that:

- There is only one energy field.
- Everything in our life is our creation.
- There is no in here (ourselves) and an out there (external events, external people), it is all just one.

- We either act based on past energy, memories (very limiting) or we act on new energy, current creation, current inspiration (so freeing and expansive).
- Everything is our responsibility.

That's it in a nutshell. It goes deep though. How do you feel about those principles which are both spiritual and scientific? In fact, quantum physics does show us that there is indeed only one energy field. Neuroscience also teaches us that most of our neurological connections in our brain are indeed based on the past and memories and it takes willingness to create new ones, different ones based on future potentiality.

The practise is to say sincerely, meaningfully those four simple yet profound sentences:

I am sorry (for whatever is causing you distress or causing someone else pain or to the general suffering in the world).

Please forgive me (to the field, Source, yourself or another... it is all one. As long as you realise nothing is external from you).

Thank you (to that one unique field of energy, to yourself as the creator, to anything).

I love you (to that one unique field of energy, to yourself as the creator, to everything).

Ho'oponopono became world famous, in recent years, as this Hawaiian doctor (Dr Hew Len) cleared a hospital from mentally severely ill criminals in three or four years. He never met anybody; he just recited the prayer in the basement of the hospital. True story! It gives hope. Then this American author Joe Vitale heard about that story, and they wrote a book together that propelled the knowledge of this powerhouse practise into the wide world. They called their book "Zero Limits". What a title!

I have been using it on my body. I have asked my uterus for forgiveness and little miracles have manifested. The most important shift is that I am feeling much more love for myself, Scarlet and life. It feels wonderful.

I want to ask you a question. Do you fully trust yourself, or are there parts of yourself you don't trust?

I came to realise that I do not trust and have feared angry Suzanne. I did not trust anger in me as in the past it made me act abruptly and irrationally, often towards Scarlet, which I am very sorry for (am sorry, please forgive me, thank you, I love you). Last week, so much anger emerged about my body. I did not know what to do with that intensity of anger. Using the Ho'oponopono prayer I started to tell my anger "I love you", it was brilliant. I actually felt energised by my anger and empowered. I could love angry Suzanne! Well this is pretty cool as I have been afraid of her for years.

Now I want to tell you about my life so you get a picture of who I am.

I was born in a tiny rural town by the foothill of the Alps. I was born a month too early and I was pretty petite which I am still! :-)

I don't have many memories of my early childhood, so we jump until I am around six onwards. Now looking back, I think that I probably observed a lot and was highly sensitive. I grew to be introvert, shy and my inner world was more important and richer than the outer world. As you know we lived by the mountains and one thing I really adored was walking there. I loved the landscapes, the air, the flowers, the eagles, the groundhogs, the silence, the torrents and their freezing cold water. Those were probably my favourite times although physically challenging too. I did not enjoy skiing that much. As I was skinny, I would get easily cold and tired. But I loved the snow. I have a passion for landscapes covered in snow and the pure silence that goes with them. But skiing was not fully my thing. My dad, at the time worked in the ski business so you can imagine what we did go a lot!

My brother Guy is five years older than me and Katy was eight, nearly nine years older.

When I was young my brother had a severe kidney condition, life threatening and he spent over one year in hospital, nearly two years at home in a hospital bed with daily injections of penicillin, then he lived another year in a children's recovery centre in an area of France where the climate is mild and stable. Hence, we did not bond normally. And then one day, he came back home healthy and I had a big brother. We fought a lot!

I think that I worshiped Katy. She must have taken quite a motherly role with me, being nearly nine years older, plus with our mum intensively involved with Guy's health. I can tell by old photos that even when I was born Katy was there as my big sister. :-)

We were pretty well off and my dad owned a sailing boat so in the summer we would go sailing in Brittany. Again, I did not really enjoy it. I loved the sea and still do but it also frightened me. Lots of things scared me as a child: loud noises, heavy agricultural machinery, thunderstorms...

Before I carry on with my life story, I need to tell you that I feel vulnerable doing this. I am exposing myself to your judgements. But it feels important that I do this nonetheless.

When I was eleven, we moved from the Alps to the suburbs of Paris. I missed nature, felt fearful of the urban environment but most importantly for me, Katy did not make the move with us. She stayed in Grenoble to go to university. So suddenly my sister was missing in my life. Also, the relationship between my mum and dad completely collapsed and they were verbally violent. My dad left home after a couple of years.

Later, my brother went to study in England, so it was only me and mum (who was depressed by then) in this big empty house. I became even more introverted, self-contained. I became acutely aware of the pain in the world, injustice, wars and it would literally freeze me.

Then at seventeen, I met a friend of a friend (he was nineteen), I took one glance at him and it was like I knew him, knew that I was connected to him on a deeper level. I ended up jumping up and down in a frenzy in my friend's kitchen. Within weeks, I had left school, my home and we were living a nomadic life travelling France on a motorbike!

A year and a half later, we were married. I was eighteen! We were together for six years until his suicide. Those six years became the most destructive and violent years of my life. I lost all sense of my self-worth, my identity and my self-esteem. I forgot who Suzanne was.

Xavier was an extremely talented musician. So, I moved from my cocoon with my mum to being with musicians who took drugs. Sex and drugs and Rock'n Roll, yeah! Xavier had already attempted suicide in his teens. His forearms were covered with deep scars where he had cut his veins. Not nice. He had had experiences of astral travel and he would tell me stories about his out of body journeys. For some reason, I believed him even if in those days, I had never read books about such things or heard of such matters. Since then, I have had my own out of body trips. But back then, I simply knew everything he told me was real.

Slowly but surely, as the years passed, Xavier's demons re-surfaced. He was eventually diagnosed schizophrenic, but I knew there was more to it. He was spiritually disturbed by living in our earthly dimension. The last two years of his life were hell with lots of self-destructive behaviour and madness. He would repeatedly sexually humiliate me. At one point, he strangled me. I remained hyper calm inside during that moment. I remember extremely clearly how I kept looking straight at him, directly gazing into his eyes. Then suddenly, he let go of his grip. I silently walked out of the flat and that was the last time we lived together. I only saw him a few more times after that shocking interaction until he killed himself a few months later.

After I left that day, he destroyed everything in our flat and ended up admitting himself to a psychiatric hospital. I visited him there once. He was drugged up on medication and different: bloated and chemically calm. It was disturbing and traumatic.

After I left him, I lived in fear, had all sorts of physical and emotional imbalances which lasted for years and affected my health.

My parents decided that it would be best for me to have a change of scenery for a while, and they bought me a plane ticket to go and live in Haiti with Katy and Michael (her Haitian husband who I now call my soul brother as he died in the 2010 earthquake after being buried alive for over two days and two nights). The week before I was due to leave for Haiti, I started shaking constantly because I knew with all my being that Xavier was going to die. By then, it was weeks we had no more contact and divorce procedures had started. Then one morning I woke up early, went back to sleep and had my first clairvoyant experience. I perceived and saw Xavier's field shift, shrink and merge to be one with the Greater Field – Source. Before he merged, his energy came slamming into mine in a rather brutal manner. I fell asleep again until I heard the phone ring. Still in bed, I knew that sound was the call to tell me that he had died. And it was. That morning, he had gassed himself to death.

I am in a distressed state writing all this.

A few days later I was in Haiti, a total emotional wreck. I could not make sense of my vision of his death, but I knew I had seen the moment of his transition. The trauma of our last two years together and his suicide were a lot for me to cope with, I ended up being skin and bones.

I had several more visions of him on the other side of the veil. I even heard cosmic music from other dimensions linked to where he was by then.

Being in Haiti overwhelmed me with a massive culture shock. The only truly wonderful thing was living and being with Katy and Michael. I lived with them for six months. Katy was the only person I felt I could share my "weird" experiences with.

When I came back, I went to live in England as I did not want to be in France anymore. I ended up six years in the UK. My traumas were never addressed, I just carried on as I could. I received some holistic therapy and body work. I became a Buddhist and I experienced a past life memory when I heard chanting for the first time. During those years, I had many past life connections that would appear spontaneously. It seems that the traumas of Xavier's life and death had opened doors for my sensitivity to access other dimensions of existence.

I was a practising Nichiren Shoshu Buddhist for nineteen years, chanting daily (well nearly), until Katy died. Buddhism made sense to me about life and death. It took me many years to stop having panic attacks and be "normal" in social settings. I went on to study plants, botany and conservation. I was back with my love for nature. I ended up studying and working for three years in the Royal Botanic Gardens Kew in London which is a worldwide top scientific institution. Those were some of the best years of my life although intensively laborious: as besides studying full-time we also worked full-time in the garden! So, non-stop work for three whole years. Kew is a gorgeous place and being everyday among the most stunning plants proved to be healing. I started to regain my self-value, self-esteem and a sense of who I was blossoming into. I was regaining my life.

At the end of my three years at Kew and graduating successfully I won a bursary to go and work in, yes, Haiti! I was to start setting up a botanic garden there with an organisation called Botanic Gardens Conservation International. An exciting project and it meant being with Katy and Michael again. By then, I hadn't seen them in seven years.

It was amazing to be reunited but the situation in Haiti had gotten far worse. The poverty had increased, political unrest, violence, curfews. I was shocked and distressed at the state of the country. By now, there were hundreds of street kids, slums, overpopulation in Port-au-Prince where I lived. After six months or so, the project fell apart as the area of the "botanic garden to be" was invaded by armed gangs and we were threatened at gun point. My colleague went back to the UK but I stayed with Katy and Michael. By then they had two sons. I did lots of different jobs in conservation and environmental education. I loved it. Katy became a Buddhist and we joined the only Buddhist group in the country and befriended many young people mostly from slums.

Although it was tough living in such a poor, degraded, and unstable country, I profoundly loved it. I got drawn into the music scene. I was also working a lot with Michael who was involved with many grassroot projects and democratic politics. I spoke the language Creole so I could communicate with everybody. I travelled on my own and went to voodoo ceremonies alone. I felt at ease and immersed myself in the culture. I have seen the dead bodies_of murdered people who are left on the streets. I walked on piles of garbage that are so high that they form areas where people live and work. The stench was absolutely unbelievable. At night, there were gunshots, and I would lay petrified in my bed. I hated the level of insecurity. One night there was a small earthquake. I could have never but never imagined that a few years later, Michael would die buried alive for nearly two days and two nights in the 2010 earthquake.

After three years there or so, I felt that my life was getting stuck and sucked by Haiti and that I should move on with my life. I relied on Katy and Michael a lot and went through phases of depression due to Haiti's general state. Sometimes, I would not leave the house for several days as I could not cope with the utmost, general degradation, the horrendous stench. I started to search for a job in a botanic garden somewhere else in the Caribbean. Then I met Michael's cousin and fell quickly in love with him. He is Scarlet's dad.

I am going to stop this letter here. I can't overload you with the story of my fifty years of Planet Blue!

I am grateful for having you in my life. Thanks. OK, Amigo Roberto.

Suzanne

P.S. This morning during my walk, I found such a beautiful perfect feather that I picked it up for you, but I thought that maybe I am not allowed to post it to you. Can I? I will wait until you tell me.

April 22nd, 2015

Hello Suzanne,

How are you doing today? As for me, I am doing alright. Things have been hectic the last few days. Nothing to worry about.

Have I made peace with my past? I can't say it is peace. I have accepted my past. I don't think I can truly make peace with it. I either accept or make excuses for it. For a long time, this is what I did, I made excuses like "all I went through made me who I was. I didn't have a choice." But the reality is that I created my past. I can say that because before being locked in this place, I made decisions that brought me to this place. A lot of people have had worst past and they are not in my situation. I shaped my choices.

Now I want to learn from my earlier experiences and help others. I accept that the choices I made led me to where I am. I used to believe that my past, the pain I went through and the feelings of abandonment were who I was. Because of my pain I have hurt a lot of people and took three lives. I used to justify those choices by making excuses for myself. I am on death row and I still have a long journey ahead.

I can't contact the families of my victims to ask for their forgiveness or show my remorse. I can't do that. Only they could contact me if they wanted.

My killings were something to brag about: "Look how big and bad I am". As I started to learn more about myself and deal with my past I began to realise how idiotic something like bragging is. The truth, the reality is that I am responsible for three people's death. I was so selfish that I didn't allow three spirits to grow. I deprived them of gaining knowledge, of building families—of living.

I am mortified.

I know that I will have to deal with those actions even in my next lifetime(s), so I want to make a difference now. It won't ever counterbalance what I have done but it will help others.

My punishment, the death penalty is the worst type of torture. It lasts twenty to twenty-five years and it is torture for the individual who is going to be executed but also for their families and especially for the families of the victims because they are forever reminded of the crime.

The cruelty and persecution is knowing that you will be killed after being locked up for twenty-five odd years of isolation and deprived of any normal human contact. We stay here caged up, not able to go anywhere except for when we are handcuffed and are moved to the caged recreation pens or showers. We live, eat and sleep all in one little box while our legal cases are drawn out and our families are put through stress at each court procedure.

All the while, we sit in our boxes contemplating our death. Although we have items to distract us, we can't help but dwell on our future. For most, the idea of our execution is horrifying, and even I, I am scared. I fear the unknown and the question of will the execution be painful? I worry about my mother and how she will react.

One of the worst parts and I consider it as the most severe ways to torture someone, is to deny them human touch: the comfort of a handshake or a hug. Touch denied can dehumanize someone.

I think about the current state of the lethal injection in the US. Death row prisons can't find the drugs necessary to execute people so we become guinea pigs. They test their execution methods and drugs on us.

It is also torment for the victims' families because for every denied appeal they are forever reminded of the murder. Some say that they feel closure after the murderer is executed but more often than not, it is only temporary closure because their execution did not bring back their loved one. This, in a way, continues a false cycle of revenge.

I would love to be able to breathe fresh air. I can only when I go outside to the recreation pens. From my cell, I can see a corner of the sky as I have a skyline window. I see the sky when I am in the pens, but there is the cage roof, a reminder that I am locked up. There are days they'll take us out at 6.15am and we can actually see the moon. And it is amazing to see it.

Reading about your different meditation practises, I now understand that in doing mine I am releasing endorphins. This explains why I feel so energised afterwards. The heart-based meditation is one I should do. I know what chakras are. If I am not mistaken chakras are the energy centres we generate and this energy surrounds us at all times. Can you fully explain how you do the heart-based meditation? I must definitely practise this. I, of course, would like to know more about bringing myself into nothingness through meditation.

As you tell me about your experience of when your sister Katy died and that you felt and saw her spirit, I felt so happy to hear about that. I know a lot of people who would want to have that. And you say it changed your destiny. I think that Katy recognised that you were hurting and knew that you needed to see and feel her in order to know that she was in a peaceful place. I am so glad that you were able to be subjected to such an event.

Mi amiga, that's it for this letter. I hope you are well and healing quickly and I hope to hear from you soon so until then please take care of yourself and be safe.

Robert

Sabado dos Mayo 2015.

Is this correct? I think maybe secundo?

Hi :-)

Just received your letter. That's great to get so much in one go. Thanks. Quite a few things made me laugh. I think that you have a great sense of humour and I also had tears of sadness and felt deeply touched. It is 11.30am here, Scarlet is still sleeping, I was up at 8am, had breakfast then did some yogic breathing and then went back to bed and slept real deeply until 11am. The pain is starting to subside which is good beyond belief.

Since my last letter I've been sleeping like crazy, like I've been bitten by the tsetse fly! I think that sleep is part of the healing process. I also felt pretty depressed and negative a lot as I was so fed up feeling so low and restricted in my body. I stopped seeing friends for over a week as it was tiring me a lot but I saw one yesterday and it was great. Still walking slowly and with some difficulties.

I totally believe you were protected in your story of you and the fire. When I lived in Haiti, one day, I had to urgently go to the French Embassy for my passport but for some reason I could not leave the house as if a force was preventing me from leaving. I even got angry at myself as the embassy was only open in the mornings. But I could not leave the house. Then someone rushed in to announce that there had been shootings and killings in front of the French Embassy. I then understood with total bewilderment that I had been protected from another dimension of awareness.

Last May, I had a haemorrhage due to the fibroids and it was pretty traumatic as the pain was excruciating and I was bleeding like crazy. I rang some local friends and neighbours but nobody was around and Scarlet was at school. I felt that I could not cope on my own with the intensity of the pain so I asked for angelic help. The crisis lasted a couple of hours and by then my neighbour was home and she came to be with me. Anyway, the following day, in bed and still unwell from the bleeding, Couscous was lying with me and staying constantly by my side. Suddenly she looked at me or rather the space next to me as if she was seeing something she had never seen before and could not comprehend. Her eyes went mad and she hissed and puffed her fur up. I could not understand. But then I remembered that I had asked for angels to be with me. She was probably seeing them but it also freaked her out.

Another time, one summer at my dad's, my brother had to drive to a nearby town to collect someone at the train station. His youngest sons (twins) and Scarlet went with him. I sat quietly in the garden and for some reason I felt I should ask for their angelic protection. So I did. A couple of hours later, they came back. All normal. At dinner that evening, suddenly my brother says that he had to tell us that they had all escaped what should have been a fatal car accident. He did not know nor understand how they did not collide. I was dumbfounded. I did not say anything to him until much later.

So yep, I am a believer! :-) But sometimes, often in fact, I forget. I think it requires a level of sincerity which I don't always have. I most certainly forgot after my operation.

What is the content of your classes? I am glad a lawsuit was put against your unit. I feel like writing to Barack Obama! But I am not sure it would help.

It makes total sense about improving yourself and thinking of your next incarnation. I feel how each moment is so valuable: an opportunity for transformation. I am still practising the Hawaiian prayer I was telling you about and still having some freeing experiences. :-)

Is your world 100% male? Were you able to touch your wife? I understand that not to touch and be touched is a form of torture and in fact, babies who are not touched, not held physically in love and care, grow with brain underdevelopment.

When I came back home after the operation and was extremely distressed by the levels of pain, I so needed support that I was stroking my own hair, face, hands and hugged my shoulders. One of the treasures we share with Scarlet: we hug and cuddle a lot and express our love easily.

Tell me more about your mum.

Thanks for sending positive energy my way. I also have your two cards which have helped when feeling so low those last few weeks. Energy sent, energy received. :-)

Yes, tell me more about your meditation and how it rejuvenates you. I like your word: "rejuvenate".

You say you feel old but you are very young. I think that you are 38 or 39.

Back onto telling you now a bit more about my life's journey. Last time I think I ended up when I met Scarlet's dad. We were together for only ten months. Lovely man with a serious drinking problem!

At first, I was naively in love. I moved quickly to live in his house up in the mountains where the temperatures were less tropical. I enjoyed his aliveness. But I soon realised that he had a tendency to drink and smoke joints daily. In all fairness to him, both his parents and his best friend had been murdered only a couple of months before (that's Haiti for you) so he coped as he could. He was a lovely person but broken.

I began to feel burdened by his upper social class upbringing and his friends, their arrogance, thinking themselves superior to the common Haitian person, and even to me as I was not covered with gold jewellery and designer clothes as they were. They would binge drink over weekend long parties to forget the reality of the country. It was an eye opener.

I eventually stopped going to those parties and he would come back home severely drunk. I fell pregnant after about four months of being together. It was not planned but I was deeply happy and excited to be pregnant. By then our connection was strained as we did not have much in common onto which build a proper relationship. On top of that, he was continuously being licentious with other women.

One late evening, driving from dinner at some of his usual friends, on a deserted mountain road and drunk he created a stupid and volatile argument with a lone truck driver driving women to the capital's markets. Since they were black poor people whilst he was a rich mulatto, it was not a situation to create tension, in a country with aggravated social unrest. I got out of the car, with my pregnant belly and gave a respectful and sincere apology to the driver, in my best creole. I stopped a situation which could have ended up much worse with machetes. Instead of thanking me, he got furious and yelled at me for a long time.

That night, knowing my baby inside of me and how this man, her so called father, had potentially endangered both of our lives, I felt a deep strength emerge from an instinctual, primal, motherly life force which overtook me. The next morning, I moved out of his house and left our unhealthy and damaging relationship. This primal awakening as I was becoming a mother has never left me since. I gained a new level of self-honouring, self-respect, self-care that led me to become romantically and sexually discerning.

After two months of soul searching, I left Haiti, hence Katy and Michael too. With Katy, we knew that this was the end of us living together as adults. It broke our hearts and souls beyond what you can imagine. I only saw her three more times before she died.

I left Haiti, seven months pregnant (huge!) and arrived in France. I went to live with my mum. We, baby Scarlet and myself, stayed at my mum's for over four years. A blessing that my mum was so open and willing to support us, but it was also challenging as my mum is a strong personality and I sometimes felt crushed by her. For the first three years I was studying, distance learning, for a Master of Science in Education for Sustainability, which I got with merit! We struggled financially as, by then, my parents were divorced for a very long time and my mum did not have that much money. I had a few odd jobs during that time but nothing major. Sometimes, just buying food was a struggle. But I cannot thank my mum enough as being a single mum is really tough! She and Scarlet also forged a strong bond of love which they still share and nourish.

When Scarlet was four, I started looking for jobs in England in my botanical and conservation field and quickly landed a great, full-time job, well paid and interesting. I was manager of an environmental education project within a charity involved in planting trees in urban areas. Off we went to live in London. This is when the reality of being a single mum hit me and us two. It was very hard to say the least. After one year of full-time work, being a full-time single mum, I started to feel unwell and ill most of the time.

I asked to work only four days a week which my boss accepted. I had grown to dislike my job. My colleagues were not that pleasant, all much younger than me and I didn't feel that I belonged in that organisation. My relationship with Scarlet grew strained due to my exhaustion and stress. After six months I lost that job which was a real blessing in disguise. I quickly found my best job ever: three days a week, lovely people, lovely organisation and even better paid. My boss of that time is still a friend. It was in North London which meant nearly three hours of public transport a day. I convinced myself that I would cope plus the salary was a real motivator. I was managing a project involving 10 different charities in deprived areas of London. I loved it.

After nearly one year and a half, at work one day, an odd fever landed on me. I had a high temperature and sore throat for two weeks. But strangely I did not recover. That was the start of being unwell for an awfully long time. After four months, I was finally diagnosed with M.E. which stands for Myalgic Encephalomyelitis. By then, I could not walk anymore, I laid in bed day and night, even holding a cup of tea was challenging. I could not wash myself properly, I lost weight. But my biggest challenge was that I felt constant pain in my muscles, in my body and in my head. That level of pain lasted for about five years.

M.E. is a chronic illness hence nobody knew how I was going to evolve. There is no known cure in modern medicine. It feels strange to think again of that time of my life. That was eight years ago. My mum, already in her mid-seventies, came to live with us as I was incapable of being a mum to Scarlet. I could not cook, read, listen to music or watch films. Noises, light and movements were challenging. Scarlet and I became close again as I was always in bed or on the sofa, so we had plenty of time being together when she was not at school.

My boss, an exceptional woman, came to visit a few times to cheer me up and check on the possibility of me returning to work, always with flowers, even a vase once and other goodies! I eventually lost my job and cried and cried for my loss. My colleagues offered me a silver bracelet with gold letters saying "Om mani padme om" written in Sanskrit. It is an extremely beautiful piece of jewellery, a treasured possession of mine. The sacred OM again! Remember?

My social life disappeared. I could not chant anymore my Buddhist practise.

I could not even look at myself anymore in the mirror. I looked dreadful. After two years, I remember it well, all of a sudden, I could look at myself and be fine with my image.

I have to tell you that I am a professional sky and clouds gazer! I have spent days, weeks, months when the only thing I could do was to look at the sky and clouds. I have seen all shapes of clouds and some are perfect. The most striking one I can remember was a cloud shaped like an old woman with a dragon on her shoulder. It was incredibly perfect with all the details. Maybe it was a sign of me from when I will be old! :-)

I am going to rest now until dinner with Scarlet.

Hey! I like your mirror description. Thank you for your honesty. I did not imagine you with a moustache! But now that I know it, it makes sense: the Latino in you. :-) What you said about feeling old, I think I understand, in the sense that the effects of being on death row must be ageing. When I lived in Haiti, Katy used to say that one year there was the equivalent of three in France because life was so intense and harsh. So, I understand you.

Before I carry on with my life's journey, I have to say that I feel a bit vulnerable again. **:-)** This is the first time I share my life's story like that with someone and in writing—an unusual and interesting experience. Thanks for the opportunity and I hope it is OK for you to receive so much about me.

Back to when I had M.E. I started to have severe sensory disturbances. At night, I would start to pulsate so fast that I could not move my body. It would start the process of having out-of-body experiences. It felt I was moving at an extraordinarily fast pace and I would detach from my body out of my head. I felt sucked by a vortex a few metres from my head. The vibration and speed were so strong that I did not really enjoy those moments. I would systematically block the process with the power of my mind as I feared having a full out-of-body experience. Have you had such moments yourself?

Furthermore, my sense of sight started to shift and sometimes I could not see things properly but only as a vibrating mass. Then when my eyes were closed, I had this constant show of colours. It would also happen when I was trying to fall asleep which made it difficult and annoying! I noticed that the colours would intensify if I received healing so after a while I refused to receive any as it was too much to cope with. At the time, I did not understand that it was my third eye chakra overriding my eyesight. This is my comprehension of it now anyway.

I started to feel my energy body or aura. It brought back the memories of me feeling this when I was very young. I had lost those memories. As a young girl, I could feel my energy body and it was much bigger than my physical body. This used to puzzle me a lot. I could see my skin but often felt at least 30 centimetres bigger and sometimes as big as my room!

Those memories made me realise how much I had suppressed my sensitivity which is obviously beyond the norm. I was feeling the continuity between myself, the rest of life and the universe as I could sense only one vibrating landscape. As a result, I touched peace, bliss and awe. I was, in physical pain, incapable of walking, had to

Sharing Our Life Journeys

hold myself to the walls and furniture, distressed by my medical condition on one level and in bliss at the same time.

I am going to stop here for now. Awaiting your next letter eagerly. :-)

Tell me about films, things you read, experiences you have had in the last few weeks.

Sending you some of the wonderfully alive green energy from all the emerging tree leaves.

Suzanne

"I love you, I am sorry, Please forgive me, Thank you". To the Divine in all and everything.

P.S. Are your letters (in and out) checked by the prison?

May 7th 2015

Hello Suzanne,

Hey there! How are things going over there? As for here, I am doing good. I've been to the nurse station twice. The first trip was to get an update on some blood test that was taken some months ago. The second trip was to try to get an issue I have with my hip fixed. It's probably going to take a fight because I need surgery.

Thank you, thank you so much for your trust in telling me about your life. In reading what you wrote I must admit it gave me mixed feelings. I am hurting for you, for all the chaos you have had to go through, the pain that you felt through the suicide of Xavier, Katy and Michael's deaths and the absence of your brother and father. You have had to go through so many emotions.

I see we have another connection as I too have a link to Haiti.

I also see your early years were filled with love and that you were growing up in a small place. I smile as I hear you were shy and an introvert as it reminds me of myself. Even now, I am quiet and only a chatterbox with those I like.

I must honestly admit that I am a bit envious as from a young adult age you were able to get in touch with some spirituality. As I learn more about energy and our connection to it, the more I want to learn. I didn't get in contact with that part of myself until I was 29 years old. I learnt about spirituality by going through life. So, I am grateful to have you in my life as I believe I can learn a lot from you and I hope you can learn from me.

I want to start with my life story. I will tell you mostly things that affected me. My earliest memory is when I was three or four years old. I was having a Seven Up soda in the evening and later that night I woke up from a nightmare and ended up crawling to my mom's room, but I was dizzy and disorientated. I was banging into the hallway walls. This is my first experience of being drunk

Years later in 2007, after a meditation, I was able to remember my stepfather of the time pouring alcohol into my soda can. Before that insight, I had only assumed he had, because I could remember seeing a bottle of Seagram 7 on the table.

My next memories were of a different stepfather around the ages of six to nine years old. He was violent and a drunkard. He'd come home and hit my mom and find an excuse to hit me and my brothers. Those years were hell as we were beaten with the cord of an iron. The beatings were done when he was mad. He'd take the iron, hold the handle in one hand and the cord in the other and he'd swing it at our butts but because of the pain we'd end up moving and the cord would hit our lower back leaving marks. Whatever he could use he would hit us with. It was not until his brother decided it would be funny to see what it would be like to cut a chilli pepper and rub it on my baby brother's anus, only then did my mum decide to leave him.

It wasn't long before she had another man, but this guy was different. He treated me and my brothers as though we were his own. It was the first time we had a positive father figure. Things went well the first two years, but he found out that he had stomach cancer and we had no health insurance, so his solution was to kill himself. He was found at his sister's house and his suicide note was on a Polaroid photo of me, my brothers, my mom and him.

My mom was devastated. For me, as a 11 year old boy I couldn't truly understand and so I blamed myself. Because I didn't know about his leaving note, in my mind I thought I wasn't a good enough son. I couldn't talk to my mom. She escaped by drinking and taking prescription pills. His death destroyed her.

I ended up getting close to my late stepfather's best friend. It was a relief as I could talk to him, be open and express how I was feeling lonely and abandoned. He was a shoulder for me to lean on—at least this is what I thought. At some point he started asking me if I had a girlfriend, later leading into questions about how much I knew about sex. Then joking about sex. I later found out that these three months were his grooming months as most paedophiles have those periods. Within two months he started to show me pornographic magazines.

Then, the day of the rape happened. It was a weird day as we were watching wrestling on television. Then he grabbed me and started to wrestle with me, but his hands were roaming all over my body. I got uncomfortable and tried to make an excuse to leave. He then got up and told me to wait. He grabbed his wallet and pulled out $20 and showed it to me and asked if I'd get naked for $20. I told him I had to go. As I walked to the door he grabbed my wrist and threw me on the bed and pinned me down so my stomach was on the bed. I tried to get free and yelled at him to let me go. He grabbed a pillow and put it over the back of my head. I struggled to breathe and as I tried to catch my breath he reached under me to unbutton my pants and pulled them down along with my underwear. I got really scared not being able to see what he was doing. Then I heard him spit, felt the pillow weighing on me again as he put pressure to it.

I felt something begin to spread my butt cheeks apart and felt a pressure at my anus. Then a slow pushing until I screamed from the pain of being penetrated. I could feel his two hands on the pillow as he thrusted into me. I became numb and lost all sense of myself. Then I felt him come inside of me. He stayed on top of me without moving for what seemed like forever, then pulled himself out of me and removed the pillow. I felt helpless and defeated. I was weak. I couldn't even stop him.

After he pulled his pants up, he told me to go to the toilet and shit. Like a robot, I did as I was told. He made sure I used a wet cloth to wipe my ass. When I pulled my pants and went into the room, he was sitting on the bed and tried to give me the money. I wouldn't take it so he shoved it in my front right pocket and sat back like nothing happened. I bolted for the door and he tried to catch me but I was out before he got up.

I didn't know what to do. I couldn't tell my mum because she had passed out, drunk, so I ended up going to my room and hid in a closet. In the span of three months and a half, the two men who had been for me idols hurt me the most. One killed himself and left me and the other raped me.

The closet was a refuge. I didn't have to be seen, others couldn't see how weak I had been. I hated myself in that closet and that was when I decided I would never let anyone hurt me— ever again.

I swore it. I swore no man would ever hurt me again and I have never had a close friend who is male since. They have all been women.

When I got out of the closet, I was angry to the point that all I felt was rage. I was dwelling, crying and beating myself up for being so weak and helpless that I couldn't stop this assault. I was mad at myself for being so vulnerable, so I vowed I would never be a victim again.

I began to get angry at the smallest things. I got into fights at school if someone touched me. I began stealing and smoking cigarettes. I stole money from my mom and her new boyfriend. I got mad at a kid who cut in line at an arcade game. I was in such a rage, I grabbed my lighter and lit the hair on the back of his head on fire. I got arrested for theft, aggravated assault and vandalism. I lashed out at everyone and became a solitary person, never trusting anyone and wanting the rest of the world to feel pain and helpless as I was.

By the time I was 12, I had a criminal history.

The man who raped me after Jon's suicide was never arrested. My mom knows now but she didn't find out until I was arrested and put on death row. I told her then. The man is no longer alive. He had a heart attack and died alone in his apartment. From what I heard he was dead close to a week before he was found. He apparently didn't have many friends and they only noticed after he didn't pay his rent. I am trying to forgive him but it is still hard sometimes. I hate that he stole my innocence and took advantage of my vulnerability after my loss.

My mom eventually got back together with my little brother's father, the one who got me drunk at four years old. She also had a best friend who had a son a few years younger, so I'd go over with my mom and play with her son. I ended up staying the night there a lot.

I slept in her son's bedroom. Once, I got up to go to the bathroom and as I was going back to the room, I saw that the TV was on. I started to go to the living room to see what was going on. I heard moaning, so I stopped and approached slowly, peaking around the corner. I saw her on the couch. She had a night shirt on and her hand was down her panties. She looked over at me startled but called me over and asked if I had seen what was on the TV before. When I said no she told me to sit down and she draped her legs on my lap. Being full of testosterone I couldn't hide my excitement and it poked her leg. She sat up and said she could help me with that and kissed me, placing her hand on my lap.

That is how it all began. I was 12 and she, in her 30s.

My mom knows now but does not know who it was. I won't tell her and her son doesn't know either.

The second time I stayed there, she complained about her feet and asked if I would massage them. Being full of hormones I got worked up. Later that night I used the restroom and she was watching a porn movie. From then on whenever I stayed the night I would have sex with her. She was like a teacher, I know now that this shouldn't have happened but back then I was walking around with my chest up.

By the time I was 13, I had been arrested for breaking into a property and charged for minor in consumption of alcohol. I was sentenced to a youth rehabilitation centre for troubled teens. I was there for nine months and got kicked out for not wanting to work with their program.

By then, my mom had moved to a Southern state so I ended up going there. At 14, I met some gang members and joined their gang. I was selling little purple pills for them. My mom once found the bag they were in and she told my parole officer. I was given a choice to go to a youth prison or drug rehab. I decided rehab, so I spent five months at a Drug Rehabilitation Centre.

I faked my way through the program. Instead of getting treatment I started doing "sherm". This is a cigarette or joint dipped in embalming fluid, the chemical that morticians use to preserve a dead body.

Embalming fluid can be used as a drug. I would get it from a gang. The effects are different for everyone who uses it. For me, it slowed me down and made me feel like I was moving in slow motion with my whole body tingling. Sometimes I would feel no pain or I would feel I was just floating. This became my drug of choice.

I had been out for four months before I was found guilty of misconduct with a minor. I was sentenced to a different rehabilitation centre for troubled youth. I was 14 years old.

It was similar to the first one, so I thought I could fake my way through. I already knew how the program worked, so I thought if I just acted like I was good and did everything the program required, I could get out and not change. And I almost did. When I was close to finishing the program, I tried to impress a girl by lying and got caught. A letter was found and when I was confronted, I became violent. For the next eight months I remained stubborn and violent and refused to follow their program. On the eighth month I realised they weren't going to just kick me out so I started working at it. It took another eight months to get through it.

Altogether I was there for 23 months, not counting the time I was in juvenile detention waiting for trial. After I came out, I did good for a few months but got back with the guys from my gang. I started drinking and getting high again.

By the time I was 18, I would stay with family, still causing trouble, so they'd kick me out. By the age of 19, I had burnt every bridge with all my family members. I had lost all connection with anyone who could help me or give me a place to stay. I ended up homeless.

I would occasionally go to hotel parties, this is when we got someone who was 21 years old or older to rent a hotel room as a place to have a party. They also bought the alcohol. A bunch of people would show up. I had started going to those kinds of parties when I was 14.

There was lots of drug use, no sex and it was full of other young people just looking to get high, drunk or have a good time.

One day I asked a guy named Peter if he would rent a room for us to party. Everyone would leave by midnight, so he agreed as long as he could stay in the room after everyone left. His wife Lily, a friend called Roland and his stepson would stay there too. After the party, we talked for about an hour and I got to know them. Arthur was a shy teenager. I explained to them that I was pretty much living from friend to friend, from party to party. Somehow the topic came up that I could stay with them. They described their property layout and I told them I'd show up in a few days. I sat back and watched television as Lily and Peter went to take a shower together.

A little after 2.30am Roland showed up. He rubbed me the wrong way because he was grumpy and had an attitude. I went to sleep and was woken up by the maid knocking on the door saying it was time to check out.

Later that day, I ran into Peter again. He said that if I was going to stay with them, I should know about the relationship between Lily, himself and Roland. He told me he was married to Lily but that they both were her lovers. I didn't care about that, I just saw an opportunity to not have to keep moving around so much. I'd have a place to stay.

A few days later, I got to where they were living. It was five miles to the nearest town, there was no running water, no electricity.

The living conditions were deplorable, out in the middle of nowhere. No electricity meant no air conditioning and no relief from the summer heat. No running water meant no flushing the toilets or showers. There was no way to preserve food so everything was eaten right away or food was bought that didn't need to be refrigerated. Lily and Peter didn't like Arthur to be left home alone there. They constantly went to town because Peter worked at one of the casinos. They didn't want to take Arthur with them. I was stuck with him a lot and ended up looking after him.

But for me, it was a roof over my head. I started doing sherm again whilst starting to work at a restaurant. I would pay $100 towards the rent plus $200 for food. Soon I found out, when the guy renting out the property to Peter and Lily passed by that the rent was $100! I was the only one contributing to the house. The other three were using me. They also ate all the food I bought.

I became extremely angry at the deception. Unfortunately I had nowhere else to go and I was afraid to be homeless and out on the streets again so I stayed. But I began to drink more alcohol. By then, I was doing sherm nearly every day, enough to where I got paranoid.

This is when we decided to commit the crimes. We'll go into that later.

Anyway, that is my life story. I wanted to be honest so I put all I could think of. I look back now and realize how stupid I was and for a long time I blamed my stepdad and his friend who raped me for my life of crime. It took a long time for me to understand that I was to blame, and my choices were made because "I" made them. I just used the excuse that I would hurt others before I could get hurt.

I do want to quickly discuss what you wrote about making yourself vulnerable while you wrote about your life. I want to thank you for opening up and putting your trust in me. I don't know what the future holds, I hope that we grow an amazing friendship, but I give you my word that I will never mistreat or misuse the trust you have given me. Please don't ever feel that you are exposing yourself to my judgments, though I may comment on parts of your life like your husband's suicide. I will never ever make a judgment upon you. I know you as you are now: an amazing, caring and loving woman who is willing to open up to me. That is who I know now. Your past no matter how chaotic it was, made you into the person you are today.

No one should ever judge someone for what they did but should recognize who they are today.

The reality Suzanne is, who am I to judge anyone? We must all live our lives no matter if they are chaotic or if they are all peaches and cream. We don't decide our lives but it is how we deal with it that matters. I will never judge you.

Una sonrisa para mi
Amiga en la Inglaterra
Espero que duermes con
Los angeles y que tienes
Suenos maravillosas

A smile for my friend in England.
I hope you sleep
with Angels and that
You have wonderful dreams

Robert

May 4th 2015

Dear Suzanne,

Thank you for being honest as to how my journal affected you. I, of course, never want to upset you but I also don't want to lie. I wanted you to get an idea of what life is like in here. The good part though is that we are usually safe from attack compared to most other prison yards. I do hate the lack of contact or being able to play sports but as long as you are able to stay busy there is less likelihood that you'll go crazy.

If you want to know more about the prison and see a photo of me, you can look at its website.

I must admit that as I read about the Ho'oponopono prayer you came across, I began to smile. As I read I began to see a lot of what I believe. I am never good at expressing my beliefs. I only know that our spirit, life energy is reintegrated into the spirit world (the one true energy field) when we die, where it rests and gains strength to once again be introduced into this plane of existence.

We as humans only use half of our brain capacity. But I think that if we were able to build on the energy around us, we would be able to use the other half of our thinking so use newer and stronger, more intensely positive, balanced energies.

Before the row, I decided that it was easier to not deal with reality so I did drugs and it altered my perception. I fell off my path of bettering myself. I never realized that it is important to spread love and positive energy in this life, so that in my next life I am even more prepared to spread them further.

I just reread what you wrote about Ho'oponopono and I can truly put my beliefs into a clearer set of mind now. I will copy these four phrases and try to use them naturally but it will take time to get used to them.

I hope it helps me with anger. It is an amazing feeling to know how much positivity can come out of anger when you start to embrace it and use it for something positive. It can make you feel better and more empowered. There will be days or times when it is too much, as anger as an emotion is hard to embrace. Even when I am unable to embrace it totally, I can't stop trying. Anger in here is something that is dealt with everyday so when it comes to it, I don't fully trust myself. I can decide to use it to clean my cell or do some work out or put music on and draw. But then there are times when anger gets the best of me.

I killed three people out of anger.

Yet more and more I begin to see how much easier it is to accept it. By this I mean that at times my anger gets to be so bad that I yell and hit the wall. I am working on this and have made a lot of progress. I have been able to welcome it more and channel it into something positive whereas in the past I did not know how, so it would explode.

Another part of me I don't trust is my heart. Mostly because I fall in love too easily. I am trying to do better though.

I do want to touch on one part of what you wrote regarding you not having been able to always control your anger and lashing out at your daughter. I want to ask you to do something for me. When your thoughts of those angry times come up, without her knowing, sit down when she is around and just look at her. Know how much you both love each other, remember that as parents we are never perfect. We make mistakes. See how proud you are of her.

Please take care and be safe. And don't forget to smile. Robert

Wednesday 6th May 2015

Robert,

Something happened this morning. I received your letter where you mentioned a photo of you on the prison's website. As my computer was on I thought why not. I went onto the site you gave me and quickly found lots of photos of men, all looking scary (apologies for my judgement). Then I found you and your photo, looking quite young. All fine until I started to read the description next to your photo, of the three murders you are charged for. I read it and started to shake. I felt like crying.

I had to calm myself, I am listening to the sound of OM right now to write to you. I went for a walk to calm down, recited Ho'oponopono prayer and realised that my deepest emotion was sadness. Sadness for you and your two "friends" who killed with you, that your lives could have been so unloved and unsatisfied that you would do such horrors. Sadness for those three killed and for their families. Sadness for humanity not being evolved yet. I don't cry easily Robert, but I am crying now. I have been so naïve!

I feel blank, in shock and having to digest that the man I write to, share with, did those horrors 19 years ago. I can tell you that much: my humanity has been seriously challenged. I am having to see how far Suzanne is capable to not judge and honour another human being: you!

It also brought fears for my safety as I am linked to you. This is probably unreasonable but still. I am being 100% open and honest here. I can't believe how naïve I have been!

I am going to send this letter just like that and will respond to your letter in the next few days once I have digested what I have discovered as this is no small piece of information.

I remain your pen friend, but this is a turning point in our emerging friendship and in fact, it is good that it happened sooner than later.

May angels be with you, with your awareness of them. That's my prayer for you.

Suzanne

Thursday 7th May 2015

Hi Robert,

The first thing I want to say is how horrified I am that all this information about you and your fellow inmates, is public on the internet. Did you know that by directing me to your photo I would find it?

There are several ways to look at what you did: victim/victimiser, judgment to punishment which is what society mostly does and in my view is based on a limited understanding of life. Or it can be observed from the Higher Self perspective where all is divine and all are playing their unique divine part, where there are no more victims and abusers, but all are co-creators.

Yesterday evening, I imagined what the angels thought or felt towards your killings. I went into a deep meditative state and allowed myself to unfold and feel. Beings of light hold such a wider perspective and understanding than us, that they probably see the threads of energy connecting people, events and points of co-creation. This is hard for the mind to grasp.

Of course, at the level of my small self, I emotionally struggle with accepting and integrating your murders. I even feel it could give me nightmares. I recite the Hawaiian prayer. From my Higher Self, and only from my Higher Self, I wonder if at some soul level, all six people (the three killers and the three victims) had all decided, way before you incarnated, of your roles and your encounter. This would mean that from the soul perspective, you all needed your relevant experiences and your soul evolution that goes with them. Who knows? But it is an important perspective too.

One of the most powerful acts we can do, is move away from seeing ourselves as victims of our circumstances and becoming the co-creators of our life. You played your part Robert and you are still playing it.

I believe the ultimate universal force in the universe is love-consciousness. It does not judge, only brings expansion in love and consciousness. It expresses itself in myriads of ways and its frequency can be either high or low and everything in between. Fear and hatred are low frequency vibrations.

I want to tell you about my friend Porter because there is a message. I met Porter two and a half years ago in Phoenix Arizona when attending a five day meditation course led by neuroscientist Dr Joe Dispenza. We were around two hundred people from around the world. I noticed this elderly man in a wheelchair and felt drawn towards him. I went to say hello and realised in amazement that he was someone whom Dr Joe had mentioned several times in his previous workshops because Porter had had a car accident and became paralysed from his shoulders down. However, he was slowly coming out of paralysis. Dr Joe had shown us a short film of Porter able to stand up with the support of others. Joe explained that through meditation and energy work Porter was achieving the seemingly impossible. To achieve such radical change and evolution,

Porter was placing his awareness of himself as a being of energy and not as a being of matter.

During the course I became close to him. I also got to know his wife and his exceptional energy healer. Jill mends spines through energy work. She is based in Idaho. We all spent a lot of time together.

After I got back home, I received an email from Porter where he shared that when I came to say hello that morning, he recognised me as someone he had called upon from another dimension! He told me about his near-death experience. Shortly after his car crash and becoming paralysed, their son committed suicide. Losing his son was too much for him after all that had just happened, and he lost the will to live and fight for his recovery. He then contracted a pulmonary embolism, died and had a near-death experience. He met his late son who told him that he was fine, and that Porter had to come back to life and become a force and teacher for love. This is when Porter came out. From that moment, he took the decision that one day he would walk again and that his mission was to bring love on the planet.

This is where there is a message for you Robert. We are here to bring love and conscious awareness. This is why you are still alive! Death row is your opportunity to become a force of love in this lifetime. Does that make sense? No wonder you asked about the heart meditation. Do not think that things will only change for you in your next lifetime. Do it now, act now, change now! Otherwise you are the victim of death row rather than a conscious co-creator with life. Don't project your salvation for after death, now is your opportunity. Make each moment count. Everyone has to make the effort to rise above his or her little self and it is not an easy task.

Now that I know what you are charged for, I understand how difficult it is for you to find peace. The fact that you have evolved from making excuses (the victim) to accepting and taking responsibility for your actions is already major. Inner peace is possible but it requires a commitment to meditation, breath work, connecting to one's soul and spirit. This is a lifetime's journey.

You say you are prepared for death, this is wise. We should all do that. One aspect of my work is around death and dying from the perspective of consciousness.

Saturday. I am looking at my new card from you (on the chest of drawers) and this drawing is the most beautiful yet. I showed it to a friend yesterday and he had tears in his eyes thinking of you and looking at your drawing.

What do butterflies symbolise for you?

Let me tell you about the heart meditation now.

Start with placing both hands on your heart area (either your physical heart or your heart chakra) for a few moments. Become aware of your breath and your heart. You can do this at any moment of the day, ideally first thing when you wake up and just before falling asleep or when you are upset.

You can, with your eyes closed (I forgot to say) connect with feelings of love, calm, compassion, joy, forgiveness, blessed—whatever feels right for you at that moment. Make sure you breathe in and out and feel those emotions at the level of your heart. You might need to nurture sadness, grief or loneliness in that same manner if those emotions appear in you. Nurture them with love and heart energy.

You can also start to soften your physical eyes, which are closed, alongside your jaw and feel a gentle inner smile and softness in your eyes and lips whilst you still connect with your heart. Just observe what happens and simply be present to what emerges without judgment. You may do the Ho'oponopono prayer whilst being in this heart connection. You might want to visualise the colour emerald green in your heart or deep purple or the sun's bright light. There are no rules, play with what comes alive in you. Don't judge or analyse because sometimes you will feel nothing or just anger or frustration, that is fine. Just carry on, persevere.

Once you are used to those forms of heart awareness and you feel your energy shift towards something more established you can use that energy and send it to your cells and organs.

With love Suzanne

P.S. Stay with your heart energy for yourself, as a gift to yourself and your being. This is a practice for you, for the time being anyway. Later, you'll do energy heart work where you can then send it to others, the universe but right now, you are anchoring the energy and awareness of your heart inside yourself.

Robert, you are a Divine Being!
Robert, you are a Being of Light and Energy! This is your true nature.
Be blessed in that awareness and let it grow.
A hug from grey London.
Suzanne

May 12th 2015

Suzanne,

You read on the prison website that I was not a nice person. This is a part of my past I am not proud of. I was in small street gangs. I got into fights and I liked to feel the dominance. I can never deny that I was this person but please Suzanne notice the "was". I was angry at the world. I was mad. I wanted everyone else to hurt like me.

I have done a lot of stuff in my life that I am not proud of. I was stupid. If I could I would change them and do differently but I can't. All I can do is be a better person now and whenever I can help someone, I do. I know I will pay for what I did in this life and when I go into my next life. There is nothing I can or could ever do that can make up for those three deaths.

I live everyday haunted by the memories, haunted by the fact that because of me they are dead. I live with that negative energy in my life and I try to cope with that. I am not perfect and I still have times when I get mad. But the difference between then and now is I know how to control it. I know how to cope with it.

The part of my life I fear most when writing to new people is my case. I never hide it but usually wait until I am asked about it. Ironically, I sent you accidentally to a place you could read about it. You had it all thrown at you at once. For that, I am sorry.

I fear this part because I never know how someone will react. Will they still see me as the person they started writing to, the person who tried to change his life, to better himself or will they see me as what I used to be?

One of the other curses of this place is that you get a chance to think. You think about who you are and when you look in the mirror and see someone you don't like and fear, you have two choices: stop looking in the mirror or change. I have chosen to change. It is a long process and I'll never be done.

Have I made peace with my past? The answer is yes and no. I have made peace with the fact I cannot change the past and I am mostly at peace with who I am now. But I can never be at peace with the knowledge that three people lost their lives at my hand.

You said that our friendship is at a turning point. I don't know what you mean by that. Look Suzanne, I know you have had a rough life and I wouldn't blame you or be mad if you decided that it is too much for you to continue writing. I would hate it as I would lose a friend. But I hope this isn't the case.

I will wait for your next letter and if you decide that you want to quit writing and move on, then from the bottom of my heart and life energy, I wish you nothing but love, joy and happiness. You will forever have a person who is grateful to have spent even the shortest of time in your life.

Take care of yourself, be safe and may the spirits watch over and protect you.

Always with respect.

Robert

13th May 2015

My dear Robert,

I want to say that I have emotionally further integrated the information about your murders, as described on the prison's website. Yes, I would have preferred to know from your own words rather than the words of the prison, for sure, and to know within the context of your life rather than a square box on a screen with no relevance to your life before and after the killings.

I rang our coordinator and had a good chat with her. She has a lot of experience herself with her own pen friends and supporting other writers. She helped me integrate this level of information. Lifelines does offer counselling to its writers for when this kind of situation happens and for when inmates are executed. I felt heard and held. Meditating from a bigger perspective helped me accept that this is what you did.

I spoke to her about my irrational fears for my safety and she said that most new writers go through this phenomenon. I agree that this is part of my journey of befriending an inmate on death row. I am quite a fearful person on some levels and not at all on others! Interesting contradiction.

I was really touched by your words for a potential farewell as you feared me stopping our friendship.

This is the first letter I write not being at home! I walked to the town centre which normally takes me a 15 minutes' walk but today more than 30 minutes' slow walking. But I have made it. A massive, gigantic improvement! :-) It has been probably four months since I have been able to walk like this. I feel a bit dizzy now and it is almost too much to take in visually my new surroundings. But here I am, in a little quiet café which makes their own handmade chocolates. This is a rare treat, but I am having two chocolates.

Do you mind me telling you things like this while you are "stuck" in your cell? I hope it gives you a sense of freedom.

I love the way you thoroughly reply to my letters. Thanks. I enjoy picking up the thread of our communication where it was left. It takes about 10 days to two weeks for me to get your answer and feedback on each letter.

So, onto your last letter and my very heart-warming rose Mother's Day card. Gracias para mi Corazon. And Scarlet's ever so stunning card! How is your ego now? Boosted? Another little joke! I feel like playing with you for fun. I was amazed that you used coloured pens! A first.

I am touched by your words on my card. Thanks so much for celebrating me being a mum. It can be quite tough being a single mum so any support and appreciation on that front is very welcomed.

Thanks for explaining that you use stencils for your drawings. I still think that you are talented as your sensitivity comes out in them. :-)

I am glad that you feel safe where you are, this is particularly important. I want to ask you how can you improve the level of physical contact? Could you hug some of the other inmates or are you never without walls, bars, handcuffs? How can you or we put more love in your place? I read in the Ho'oponopono book that Dr Len (the Hawaiian man) used to recite the prayer literally to the walls of the prison where he worked as he felt that even the walls were starved for love! Does it sound crazy? It is mind blowing really.

I hope one day there is no more death penalty, no more wards, no more murders, no more abuse. This might take more than just one more generation. But look at what Dr Len did in Hawaii. He emptied an institution, full of severe psychopaths in just three years of blessing that place. I know, I am naïve and a visionary, but we have to stretch our beliefs into what is deemed impossible because history shows us it does become possible at some point!

As you seem to enjoy music, do you dance to it? Dancing is vitally important as it is a direct pathway to the soul and spirit. I used to go to dance sessions called the Five Rhythms. For around two hours we dance freely but what matters is just to feel the music move your soul, body and spirit. Let me see if I remember the names of those five rhythms: flow, staccato, chaos, lyrical and stillness. It starts with a slow beat, so you just flow with the music and warm up your body. Then it just goes faster and more chaotic so that you lose all control and restraint. Then it slows down again until it is nearly so slow you don't really move anymore: stillness. It is a freeing dance. Any emotion can appear and be expressed through movement: rejection, insecurity, jealousy, joy, bliss etc. I have seen people cry as we land in stillness as the entire process opens a space of peaceful liberation. It is truly beautiful and powerfully nourishing. Ti amiga Suzanne sends you this assignment to dance at least 30 minutes daily!

Does your mum feel guilty for your childhood? How does she cope with your circumstances? Does she live alone? As you probably have figured out by now, I am curious by nature!

I am glad that the Ho'oponopono prayer made you smile. I am still doing it a lot, daily and experimenting with it. So far, I like how it helps me to focus my thinking and emotions from negativity to positivity pretty quickly.

I think that you are good at expressing your beliefs. :-) Maybe you just need more practice, so you feel more confident in doing it.

Back to anger and linking it to heart meditation. We can learn to love our anger, even its scary bits. I mean really feel love and compassion for our anger. I can understand that anger is very present in your world. I am so glad that you trust yourself more with it.

You say "I don't trust my heart"! Well, I have quite a bit to say here. I think that given your life circumstances on death row, it is totally normal that you fall in love too quickly and easily as you put it. We all need the basic needs of love, human contact, care, warmth, reassurance and intimacy. You are seriously starved in body and soul. It is not a question of not trusting your heart but more understanding how starved it is. Am I offending you here? I hope not but I feel I need to check that with you.

I shared the same affliction although probably differently, but I have learnt by my numerous mistakes and through being a single mum. Thanks to my mystical experiences where I gained glimpses of divine love as a force. Those do not negate romantic love and I miss having a companion, but I have learnt to feel love, regardless of being or not in love with someone. Most importantly, I experienced loving myself through meditations and spiritual practices so this has healed my heart. I truly believe that we need to fall in love with ourselves first, then we can be in a romantic connection with someone else. Does this make sense to you?

I do not seek a romantic connection with you. As our relationship develops, we learn to care and appreciate each other. I really hope that a form of unconditional love can emerge between us. That would be awesome!

Your views on all of that, por favor.

So, tell me how much you love yourself? Who are all those people you fall in love with? Are you gay or bi-sexual? I have no problem with that. How much do you love the Divine? How much do you love life? Ah! That's another level of love: loving life regardless of its shape. Not easy. How much do you love your body and your cells?

I am going to go home now. It is around 5pm and I need to do a few concrete things once I am home. I will write later today or tomorrow.

Saturday 9am. I was so tired yesterday evening that at 8pm I was in bed. Feeling good this morning.

Thanks for your words about my parenting and Scarlet. I have done what you asked me: to look at her and yes, indeed she is a happy, balanced teenager. At this point, can I ask you about the mother of your daughter and your relationship to them? Does your daughter have brothers and sisters?

More questions: How much personal belongings are you allowed to have? Where do you keep your letters? Can you put things on your walls like photos? What is your favourite food? Ah, by the way Scarlet loves the pop-tarts you mentioned a few letters back. :-) Do you ever get to eat fresh fruit or vegetables? Are you ever ill? Do you have or receive any form of support or therapy to help you with your past and being on death row?

Do you know about shaking stress out of your body? Animals, mammals, do this (well, maybe not elephants) and birds also actually. After a stressful situation, animals give themselves a good body shake and there is a good reason for that: it removes all stress hormones from the cells. It prevents stress settling into the tissues and organs. I shake daily, very often at night, I shake for a few minutes and it really feels good and freeing. A powerful release.

It is super easy. You literally just gently or vigorously shake your arms, body, legs, head, you may even allow a sound to be shaken out of you. It is different and unique every time. Sometimes, I start with my hands and allow the movement to grow into other parts of my body. Other times, I start with my feet and ankles. There are no rules and exploring different ways is great. Give it a try and let me know how you are shaking! You might become Shaking King! :-)

This might surprise you but there are a few things I envy when I think of you. I envy you not having to cook and do the dishes! I hope you like that and it makes you smile. Having to deal with cooking and cleaning day in and day out, several times a day makes me somewhat depressed. :-)

Good news as I feel at my best since the operation, I am smiling more indeed! Thanks for your reminders. I am closing here so I can catch the Saturday morning post.

A bientôt,
Suzanne

Friends for Life

May 19th 2015

Suzanne,

Your letter and words really touched my heart. Thank you for what you said about me being a divine being.

I am sorry it took me five days to write back but I wanted to talk to my friend/sister first. I have tried to imagine what it would have been like to read what you read, to think how I would react. But I won't ever be able to think like that so I wanted to get her point of view. She has written to other people on death row before me and she is married to a man in a California prison so when she started writing to me, she already had an idea what it would be like. She is also into spirituality but it leans more to the Native American Indian one.

I must admit that your response to finding out about my charges really scared me. I was really feeling bad. I hate that I didn't know that there is a detailed description of my case on the prison's website. You got to see it without any warning. I was scared because I was afraid that you would quit writing. So to get your letter, I was really glad. I must admit I read this letter extremely slowly.

Thank you for looking at me as a person, for being willing to meditate and understand or try to understand. Thank you also for helping me with the heart prayer. Hopefully you'll be able to help me learn more and I'll help you too.

Love is a powerful emotion and that you are willing to show that to me, honors me and shows that you are well advanced in meditation. I am thankful that you are in my life.

As for what you said about me changing so that I bring love into the world from death row, I do what I can, though it is limited. I do try to better myself. If someone needs help in here, I try to help despite the typical macho mentality that exists predominantly. I am willing to talk to anyone who is respectful and not looking to cause drama if they just need an ear. Teaching them ways to meditate if they want to learn or if they are without hygiene or stamps. If I can help, I will.

Thinking and meditating about your letter which I have read and reread about 20 times or so in the last five days I can say that I never thought about love being so powerful and that it could be the essence and drive to change. The more I think about it, the more I want to learn. As I was meditating I came to the conclusion that I needed to take an extreme step towards love because of my current surroundings.

This step I will write in the next few lines is a promise to myself and an oath to those who love, support and care for me. I will also write it on a separate paper and would ask that you burn it to send it to the spirit world as my contract to everyone.

My oath is an oath of love.

I, Robert,
vow to practice the act of love upon all creatures
and to show kindness, love, and empathy
to all around me.

When I am angry or frustrated,
I will take the time to meditate
so I don't yell, disrespect, or act violent
towards anyone else.

I will do whatever is in my power
to share love with all those open to receive it
and for those who are not,
I vow to respect and show compassion.
This is my vow of love to the spirits that protect us all.

I know Suzanne, that I have to do it but I also know that to write it and burn it is a way to seal the vow. It is a huge step for me as I know I sometimes have a temper. With this vow I will be more tolerant.

Your question about my drawing of butterflies and what they symbolize for me, made me smile. You are the first person to ask this question! For me, roses and butterflies represent the power to change. First, roses, they begin as a seed and they grow to bud those beautiful flowers. Roses also symbolize love and beauty in the tenderness they represent and the softness of their petals.

Butterflies are the true essence of change. They begin as a caterpillar. They spend the first part of life eating, gaining sustenance for their bodies to prepare them for the next part of their lives. Then they find a decent place to hang their cocoon and begin their transition. For humans this cocoon and transition I believe is meditation. When they emerge from their cocoon they are butterflies: beautiful, delicate beings as they fly into their next stage.

This is us human beings. We begin our lives as caterpillars: we spend our childhood growing, gaining the sustenance and knowledge we will need for our next stage of life. Here we must decide how we

> Hello Suzanne,
> A rose to brighten your day and to make you smile. I hope that all is well and that you are in good spirits know that you are in my thoughts. Take care and be safe Don't forget to smile and always dance.
>   Con Amor Siempre
>   Robert

go forward. This requires ideally a space to retreat and cocoon oneself. For a lot of people they see it as getting on with life. For others they find their purpose in work or family and there are others who find their purpose in search for deeper knowledge and for a better life. Some even prepare themselves for their next life.

I was one of those who just got on with life. I don't know what I can do but I do want to help others so they are able to avoid pain or causing pain to others. I will try to see how I can help and find my purpose more.

I plan to do a long heart meditation tonight. The rest of the guys will be going to class so it will just be me and another guy on the floor. It will be quieter than normal. I will be able to concentrate more and won't have to wear earplugs.

The classes we take are spread out in different topics. The first I did was "socialization". We went once a week for eight weeks which is the length of all our classes. Now I am taking "responsibility thinking". We are handcuffed on our way there. Then it is pretty much, go to a classroom, we get our legs cuffed to the desk which is bolted to the ground. Our hands are free so we can shake hands but the guards frown on that. We go over a thin booklet about three or four pages. The class is one hour long.

About loneliness, we don't hug guards or inmates. We barely have physical contact except the minimal contact at class when hand shaking and having handcuffs on and off. The only other contact is if you get examined by a doctor. Yes I am handcuffed even then, but instead of behind the back, we are put on side restraints. This is a chain that goes around the waist with a handcuff on both sides of the body. Being handcuffed now is just part of daily routine but for the first five or six years it was demeaning and it made me feel depressed. I hated it but now it's just part of life.

It is a 100% male world when it comes to the inmates. There are some female guards and I know it is hard on them because of having to deal with rude people. I usually don't talk to the guards, period. It's just easier that way. I say thank you or if I need something like shower or recreation time. I am respectful. I was never able to touch my mum when she came to visit. The visits are done through a Plexiglas.

I know that lots of people out there are pro death penalty. How can it be right to execute someone with drugs that not even vets would use to put an animal to sleep with? I know there are a lot of families who lost loved ones and want revenge but if you see statistics a lot of those people who think that the revenge will give them closure realize after the execution that nothing has changed. For them the only real change is that instead of the victim's families hurting, the family of the executed is now also hurting.

My mom. Where to start? We lived pay cheque by pay cheque. My mom, for all her love, worked nonstop to provide for us. She did the best that she could. I know now that she often went without things for herself so that we could have clothes, food, Christmas presents. In the past I thought she didn't care but now I know she did, because she worked to support us so there was a roof over our heads.

Today, we are closer than we have ever been. She lives on her own. I call her about every six days. I am allowed 10 minutes and we usually talk about her, her gardening and her dog.

I started doing the heart meditation you showed me. Usually before I go to bed. I am still getting used to it. For my usual meditation, this is what I do. I place a folded blanket on the floor. I put earplugs in, so it's quiet. I sit with my back to the wall, legs outstretched. I put my hands on my thighs, palms up and I close my eyes and breathe normally. I can feel my heart beat. I think of my favorite place in the world, the waterfalls in Idaho and I put my heartbeat in rhythm with my thoughts and I am there. There I can just escape. I see the colors and the mist from the waterfall. I can walk without confinement and I can draw energy from my surroundings. This is usually for 30 to 45 minutes. Then I come back. When I get up I am reenergized. I feel rejuvenated and often can go nonstop whether it is drawing, writing or whatever my day entails. I plan when it gets hotter to meditate outside in the little recreation pen.

I feel a lot older than my age.

As for the man who helped me change 10 years ago, he gave me a poem. It did help a lot. This guy was a savior of sorts. I don't remember his real name as he went by a nickname. He was in a prison gang and had been in prison multiple times before coming to death row. He is now off the row and in a different prison. His sentence was commuted to life without parole.

Back when I first met him, I was being a knucklehead. I didn't want to look weak so if I got in an argument I would call others names and offend people. I truly cared about what others thought of me and with him having been in a prison gang, I thought he'd show me the rules of that kind of life. But he, in fact, decided to show me how to change. I showed him that I was willing to learn so he got me on the path I am now on. It took a very long time to actually feel comfortable with myself. I think the biggest hurdle was that I had to accept myself. The crazy part is that I know after all those years I have only scratched the top of the knowledge I can learn.

He was a true friend and he helped me to get over my ego. Though it is still there, I now realize I am not the only one in the universe. Talk about a huge blow to the ego.

From time to time I still get angry at small stuff or noises others do and I start to speak out but I feel a chill or my lower jaw vibrates and the sensations are so strange that the anger fades. I don't concentrate on the anger, instead I concentrate on the sensation. I think it is an energy that tries to help me with my anger.

Thank you for having told me about your battle with M.E. You didn't mention if it is a recurring illness. I couldn't imagine five years of constant pain. I see you are a strong woman.

Alright, to your questions before I close: access to self-development and spiritual books from the library, they are listed but when I tried to get some spiritual books I never got them. So I quit trying. As for windows, there are none in the cell but I can look out my cell to a skyline and look outside but it's blurry. I look at the sky when I go out to recreation.

I don't get close to people: inmates or guards. But I do have two people in here I consider true friends: Tuck is my neighbor but Eddie is in a different pod on H-clusters side. So we don't get to talk a lot. In fact, I have not seen him in nearly three years.

As for you feeling vulnerable and fearing that I might think you are a weirdo, you never have to worry about that, and hey, we are all weirdos in our own ways, like me falling in love too easily, so easily, that you won't send me a photo of yourself for fear I will fall in love.

Seriously Suzanne, thank you for opening up to me. I am glad and honored that you trust me enough to open up about your life.

Always with love and respect. Robert

Saturday 23rd May 2015. 9am

Hola mi amigo.

I am amazingly, writing in my garden, facing the sun which is already quite warm for British standards. :)

Gracias para ti lettra or is it carta? I received it Thursday and I read it whilst waiting for a hospital appointment to start physiotherapy to help my back, which is not happy at all since the operation. So, there I was reading your letter when I lifted up my head and realised that I was surrounded by people with no legs, no arms, no hands or only bits of limbs. I was shocked. I learnt afterwards that it is a national centre for rehabilitation for people with amputations! That put some relativity to my daily problems I can tell you.

Onto your letter: I am glad that you are doing good. In fact, since reading your letter, the overall feeling I get from you, is how much of a strong person and strong spirit you are. I feel the same about myself. I am impressed at how thoroughly you reply to my questions, sometimes even before I have sent them!

How was your day on your daughter's birthday? You must have been thinking of her. You have not yet mentioned her mum in your life story. What you said about learning about spirituality through life rather than in books is the best way, otherwise it is only intellectual knowledge, which is great don't get me wrong, but spiritual knowledge has to be integrated in one's life.

You say that you are grateful to have me in your life and you feel we can learn from each other. I also feel deeply grateful for knowing you, you have added depth to my daily life. I have been sharing about you and our friendship with my close friends and they are also benefiting from knowing of you through me.

Sharing Our Life Journeys 111

I don't want to sound naïve. I know that you killed three people. This was 20 years ago and this cannot be undone. That's the reality of your past and there is the "you", you have become during your 19 years on the row. In a way, this is the only real factor that can vaguely counterbalance the loss of those three lives. And yes, I have gained a lot from you. Maybe we are spiritual companions!?

I am learning through you about one of the most extreme ways to live: knowing you have killed and to live in solitary confinement with a death sentence at some point.

I am learning about your spirit. You are acting like some sort of mirror where I can observe and see my spiritual and intellectual limitations or openness. My beliefs are challenged by your very life. I can also observe my love capacity for another fellow human being who bears the labels murderer and death row inmate.

I have learnt about being disturbed by your actions, upset and touched by your abused childhood.

I am learning about myself in my commitment to you.

I am learning to be simply myself with someone who is living a radically different life.

I am learning to be the best friend I can be, through letters, to someone I might never meet, see, touch or talk to.

I want to say that my commitment to you is until the end of this lifetime. Well, there is the word "death" in "death row"! We might both decide we should part at some point. I also believe that whoever dies first and goes to the other side of the veil, will wait and welcome the other one when their time comes. Do you think this is strange?

I know I will meet Katy and Michael at the time of my passing. I have had connections with them since they both left our plane of existence and passed into the other realm we call death. I have zero doubts that we are greeted when we die. I actually saw how Katy was met and it was the grandest encounter I have ever been allowed to witness.

I believe that only the physical body dies. The rest: our spirit, soul, energy, consciousness transmutes eternally, out of linear time. It seems that you share similar beliefs from what you have told me.

Exciting news: the post has just arrived with a loud "flap" and my mum has just sent me the 8th book of the Children of the Earth. So, I am going to start the Land of the Painted Caves.

Okay, I need to stop for a bit as I need to deal with laundry, a Saturday morning ritual and order our next online grocery shopping. More later.

6pm. What a day! Post-operative pain came back. I did the Hawaiian prayer. It improved.

I want to thoroughly reply to some of your previous letters.

A difficult question: have you forgiven the man who raped you? I cannot imagine at all what 11 year old Robert felt but what comes out very strongly in your letter is that the decision you made in that closet "I swear no man will ever hurt me again", was an almighty decision which shaped your life. I can feel the power in your reaction to your grief, hurt, betrayal, but mostly your loneliness and lack of support at such a young age.

About the woman who had sex with you when you were a kid. A part of me likes when you say "she was like a teacher". It made me think of Jondalar in the Earth's Children books and his initiation with his older Doni teacher who teaches him how to give sexual pleasure to women. I was also shocked as you were so young. You were a kid! Another part of me was outraged as this is sexual abuse of a minor. This is illegal and she could have gone to jail.

The next parts of your life: the rehab centres, the sherm. I cannot imagine the level of harshness. You were again so young. It feels that you held a certain inner strength and used your own strategies to live. You were strong and yet lonely in a desert empty of adult support, love and kindness. Please tell me more about the paranoia that sherm gave you.

I also feel there was a kind of survival force inside of you which you directed towards destruction and eventually killing: a pent up rage.

You say you were stupid. I strongly disagree here. You were not stupid, you were desperate! Big difference! You did your best with what you had and knew. I totally understand your need to hurt others before you could get hurt. I think this is basic survival behaviour. You were not stupid; you were hurt and aching.

I was taken aback and touched by your words of respecting my trust in you. I think that you are the first and only person who has said that to me. :-) This is unusual to say but in the context of your life and circumstances, it makes sense and I appreciate it. Thank you. The quality of your integrity is important to me. Your words on the subject of judgment are beautiful: "who am I to judge anyone?". Thank you for your transparency here. The peaches and cream made me laugh.

You say that "we don't decide our lives". I disagree to an extent. We create our lives by virtue of our karma; and our past and most importantly current acts. It is up to us how much we evolve and ascend. Your difficulties were and are tailor made for the evolution of your consciousness. Ditto for me and anybody else. What do you think? There are no victims, only souls who have forgotten their soul agreements. You are right when you mention "it is how we deal with our lives that matters." :)

You say "I will never judge you and never hold anything against you". Those are the words of someone who is spiritually evolved. Those words are the words of someone who knows the power of being humble and who can forgive.

I would like to return to telling you about my life's journey again. I think I stopped with M.E.

Eight months into the illness, I met the lady who was to become my mentor in psychic development. She told me about a cure for M.E. called the Lightning Process which is a three-day process where you are taught techniques based on neuroscience which you apply to cure yourself.

The first day of the Lightning Process was highly challenging. It was only me and another lady with the instructor. We learnt the theory aspects and started to apply them. He told me that I had to go back home not in a taxi but using public transport which meant crossing all of London by tube. It scared me as I didn't trust my muscles anymore, nor myself or sense of direction. I managed thanks to my newfound skills and having fun imagining that I was a giant rather than nourishing my fears.

By the end of day two, my symptoms were at their worst in eleven months. I was practicing the technique every ten seconds and my thoughts were "attacking" the neurological patterns that were keeping the illness in my body. This generated an inner chaos unequalled in my life. That night, after about two hours of utter insanity of breaking neurological connections, I had a spontaneous remission!

I will always remember this unique experience. It is difficult to put it in words but imagine being in the middle of a nuclear war zone where a bomb has just exploded. You fight your way forward like a robot. Suddenly, after two hours of gruelling effort to simply stand upright in that nuclear wave, everything vanishes. You are in the same place but now it is a field of peace. That's the only way I can describe this healing. I knew with all my being that I was cured.

On the morning of the third day, I had one of the most important multidimensional experiences. I went from being in my bed to being instantly in another dimension. A desert place at the East of Egypt. There, different times merged. I could see each grain of sand, the texture of rocks as if my senses were magnified a thousand times. Everything was clearer and more real than in our usual dimension of daily life.

I was totally alone in that landscape and ended up inside a mountain cave where time split into the now, future and a distant past, all at once. I knew this place and it held vital keys to my existence. The cave was in the "now time" a museum, and its access was forbidden and blocked by a pane of glass. However, my life depended on me going inside that cave. My future Self demanding it. As this was non-negotiable, I stepped out of my physical body as a ball of energy and travelled beyond the speed of light through the pane of glass. The cave was filled with ancient mummies like the untouched inside of an Egyptian tomb in a pyramid. I was in the "past time" there. Flying from high speed to no motion, I stopped right above the face of a mummy. I knew this mummy was me! I had been this person in a faraway distant past, a few thousand years ago. I was one with it.

This is when I heard my own voice speak loud and clear as if coming from both my ancient dried-up body and my current self: "I am your spirit and I am healing you". And bang, I was in my bed in

London, stunned. I could hear the London planes above and I could not move from shock.

I was now healed and I attended the third day in a kind of trance. That afternoon when I came back home, I ran up the stairs as a statement of success of having cured myself. I had not run up the stairs in nearly one year! I still had to apply the technique for twenty-one days to fully solidify my cure. Little did I know that my morning experience in the multidimensional desert would shed light to what I would painfully live one week later.

Early that evening, I went into my bedroom and laid on my bed in order to regain my calm. Fully awake, I saw angels or beings of light partying in my room and throwing gold dust everywhere. I surrendered to this astonishing spectacle. I felt like a puppet in the hands of a giant puppeteer. I was in awe.

The next morning out of the blue we got the shattering news that Katy had just been diagnosed with acute leukemia. Katy died in three days in the same week I cured myself in also three days! I feel we were intrinsically linked at a deep level despite being geographically far apart.

I need to stop now as I feel emotionally churned from reliving those moments. More tomorrow. Buenas noches.

Sunday. Today I want to write about some of my thoughts about your spiritual role as a Divine Soul on death row. I think that you are a key factor for change to happen from within the row. Again, I am infused here by Dr Len, Joe Vitale and Ho'oponopono. I will photocopy some pages from the book to include in my letter.

Your awakening into higher levels of energy and consciousness is directly affecting positively your immediate environment and the planet as a whole. Are you aware of this? You are behind concrete walls but energetically you are one with the world and the universe.

I feel that I belong to a spiritual family of people who are aware of consciousness. You belong to this family too. I feel it is time for humanity to ascend into harmony, love, peace, compassion and creativity.

Sending this now.
Suzanne

May 23rd 2015

Hola Suzanne,

How are you feeling today? As for me I am good. Just want to respond to the letter I got a few days ago. But I have to say I was smiling when I saw how you started the letter "Hola Roberta". I love when you tease me.

First a quick update. Over here things are normal. There was a little drama on Wednesday when I went to the outside recreation pens. A guy I have had an issue with in the past and he wanted to talk about our problem, mostly ego stuff like puffing his chest out at me in front of everyone. I was proud of myself as in the past I would have gotten angry but now I didn't. It is all sorted out.

It is good to hear you stopped at a cafe that does their own chocolates and had a few, and yes it is alright to tell me things like that. About three or four weeks ago I kept seeing commercials for Milky Way candy bars and the prison sells them so I ended up buying two of them. I usually never buy them.

I am really glad that you liked the mother's day card I drew for you and yes, it feeds my over inflated ego even more! :-)

I get my information from the television but I try not to watch too much news. The real test in here is not to let the television run your day. It is easy to just sit and watch it.

You asked a lot of questions, so let me answer them one at a time. What could I do to improve the level of physical contact? There isn't anything that can be done. We almost always have some kind of barrier between us so there is never a chance that we could hug.

The classes we go to are supposed to be the start of more privileges. But the prison often starts stuff like that and changes it. We were supposed to get to play basketball but they started the test program on a different wing (not death row) and someone got killed on the first day. They took the basket away from us. We can only wait and see but for now we are stuck with how things are.

I do understand what you mean by this place being starved for love. Keep sending good energy and your letters help, probably more than you realize to put more love in here.

Thank you for the dancing assignment! I am failing at it. I have danced a few times but I felt silly. I am not a good dancer. I just have to get used to it so I will try to dance more. You mentioned the five rhythms of life, that was interesting.

My mom is 59 years old and lives by herself. She came to visit a few times over the years but the last time was in Feb 2005. I know it is hard for her to know that I am here. There is some guilt in her but it is unfounded—at least I think it is.

My mother blames herself and feels guilty because she had her problems and worked a lot so couldn't be there when I was growing up. But I know that as a parent there is always some guilt. I know she did what she could and I don't fault her for that. I do feel really terrible that I put her in the position to have a son on death row.

I have three brothers that I know and grew up with. I do not have any contact with them. My mum keeps me up to date with what is going on with them.

I didn't know my biological father when I was growing up. I wrote to him ten letters since I have been here. From him, I have a half brother and sister, but I have never met them.

Before the murders happened in 1996, I wasn't in a good spot in life. I fell off my path because I did nothing to improve myself and at the time I was self-destructive. I was lost and angry. I was busy drinking and getting high, doing whatever I could to mask and numb the pain. I never kept a job for long and never stayed in a relationship. I was so paranoid about getting hurt that I wouldn't let anyone get close to me, often sabotaging connections with friends and family members.

When I first came here in the row, I was full of hatred and blame. I would yell at people, bang on the cell front and threaten to make a homemade weapon to shoot out of the cell. I did whatever I could to make people think I was tough. The reality was that I was scared! But I let my anger and rage fuel me. I let the mask of fear overrun me. The fear of being on death row and not knowing my future was too big to bear. I didn't want to appear weak. I allowed my anger to hide my fears. It took nine years to find myself and realize all the pain I was carrying. It took that long to finally start to let go and build my self-esteem.

What you said about me not trusting my heart makes a lot of sense. I have been locked up for nearly two decades, I think it explains why I fell so quickly for my ex. I just wanted to be in love. I wanted it so bad that I overlooked the little signs.

I do think that being in here and not being able to have those basic needs of love met means I can more easily fall in love or look for it in the wrong place. By wrong I mean that I overlook the signs of low self-esteem, or someone who has emotional problems. I end up trying to be careful around that person instead of being honest or seeing that the relationship is wrong.

Your views on love are interesting. I will need to think about them but just off the top of my mind I would say that you are definitely right about us having to love ourselves first before we can love someone else. This is something I have slowly been able to learn. I have been able to understand that if I am meant to fall in love then it will happen. This is why I no longer look for love when I am writing. I try to be more conscious on what I write. I still write from the heart. I am concentrating on how I feel about myself.

As for what you said about mystical experiences regarding love, I have never experienced that so I don't think I could comment. But let me ask you this, do you consider some love connection you have had with some people as mystical ones?

Onto some more of your questions. How much do I love myself? I do love myself but not as much as I should. But I am learning.

Who are all the women I have fallen in love with? Thinking back I have fallen in love with only two women in my life. Incredibly I never slept with either and I think this is why I love them.

How much do I love the Divine? Not as much as I should but I do want to learn more about how I can love it more.

How much do I love life? This for me has been a struggle since I have been in here. For me it is hard to love this life because of what I did and being on death row. For me the most important part of my life is my daughter and I have no contact with her.

How much do I love my body? I love it but I know I need to lose weight and I have been diagnosed with a right hip slipped capital femoral epiphysis so when I move too much my hip begins to ache and the pain travels across my lower back then up to my shoulder blades. When I was first diagnosed in 2001, I was told it couldn't be fixed. I recently found out that it can be fixed by speaking to the doctor who does the updates. So I will probably end up in a battle with the prison to get the surgery but I am afraid that after 14 years it has progressed beyond any chance of being fixed. I have been on medication to alleviate the pain. But I don't like to be on constant pain killers.

As for my daughter's mom, she is one of my co-defendants, she was 14 years old at the time. I didn't know her well. When I met her, she told me she was 18. When we went on the run after the murders we started to mess around while the other guy was away.

My daughter is my only child.

Personal belongings: we are supposed to have only four boxes of 15x12x10 inches in our cell. One for clothing, one for legal papers, one religious and one store box but they never hassle us on them. I have five because I need to stack two of them to put my TV on. We are allowed one television, one walkman radio, one fan, one electric razor and one kettle. My cell is actually bare compared to others. We are allowed seven books, five magazines and ten cassettes tapes. My letters I keep in a box.

We aren't allowed to put things on the wall but as long as it is respectable, the guards don't harass us. Right now, I put up the painting you sent me of the flowers you did, a picture of my daughter and our food menu.

My favorite foods: I love spaghetti and meat sauce, I love homemade tortillas. The last time I had homemade tortillas was 20 years ago.

I had to smile as I saw that your daughter loves the Red Velvet Pop Tarts. They are good but I have to be careful because I'll end up eating more than I should. We don't get fresh fruit. You only get fresh vegetables if you are kosher so for those who are Jewish or Muslim. My neighbor is Muslim, and he'll occasionally save carrots and celery and put them in the shower so I can pick them up.

We don't get any counselling or therapy.

I have never heard of physically shaking off stress. I am curious and want to see if it'll work in here.

As for envying me on a few things like for not having to do the cooking or washing dishes, the dishes I agree with but I love to cook! And I do have to do dishes but only like one bowl and cup or on occasion I'll have to do two bowls.

I am sending a hug along with some good energy.

Love and respect. I do mean it. I don't write those words lightly.

Robert

P.S. Can you please burn my full oath of love and non-violence?

As I, Robert,

am on a spiritual and personal development path,
I do hereby pledge and vow that I am,
and will be doing all that is in my power to spend all my energy to live my life as a person of non-violence.
I am celebrating my life and the lives of others by spreading the word and actions of love and positive energy
in both my words and behavior.
I am meditating and live by the love
that I show to others and shown to me by others.
I am doing all that I can to surround myself and my environment with the positive message of love.
I am spreading it to those who are open to receive it.
I am not letting anyone else control
or have power over me through negativity.
I honor and respect others intentionally.
When I am angry or irritated, I take time by myself
to put my thoughts in order
and to place my body and mind
in a state of calmness and harmony.
I make this my pledge and vow to those people in my life and who will come into my life in the future, to the creator ultimately and most importantly to myself.

Robert

Tuesday 2nd June 2015

Dear Robert,

I have not been able to write last week. Scarlet was on holiday so I was being a busy mum. Then I had to finalise 13 months of my professional self-employed account and that took all week. I have now completed a big dossier for some financial support as I have not been able to work since last December. In the last few months, I have had to borrow money quite a bit, from friends and my dad. I urgently need money to enter my life again.

Last week I saw my surgeon and he told me that I can start to work again, only two hours per day. Not sure if I have told you that, in December I had started a job as part-time assistant manager in a local charity shop. This is to complement my self-employed work. The salary is the most basic you can get in the UK, so my ego is out of the way, but it is going to give me a rhythm and a financial base to rebuild a level of professional self-confidence. I have not worked like that since M.E. A big change for me. I feel ready.

When you say that you are haunted by what you did, I understand. At the same time, we all need to learn to let go of guilt, self-hatred, shame and self-blame, because those are low frequency vibrations. They are not based on self-love. At some point, we need to drop the crap from our past. I am not saying that this is easy, but we are here to evolve or are we not?

I am going to do some yoga now before I hit the pillow.

Thursday. Started working this morning. A very different energy from my recovery cocoon.

Your oath! I feel that I need to totally honour it by remaining a silent witness. I will burn it. I look forward to hear about your ups and downs and journey with your oath.

Interesting that you see the rose as a symbol of change. Rose essential oil is considered of high frequency. It allows a gentle opening of the heart when put on the heart chakra. You can imagine putting rose oil there, it will still affect a positive change. The power of imagination, hey.

Roses for me are simply divine. Divine flowers on earth! :-) I am lucky as maybe the weather is not brilliant in England, but this is the country par excellence for roses!

I have a proposal to make! I am on the lookout for projects to expand and enrich my life. Do you want to write a book with me? I am serious! I imagine a book that will tell its readers how we can all have the potential to overcome our challenges and make the world a better place. Our own life stories can inspire others. I feel you have a wealth of wisdom to share. What do you think? I am serious but if this feels too farfetched for you, no worries at all.

As soon as my finances are better, I will get you some books through the prison system. Tapes might be more difficult to find nowadays.

OK, this is a bit of a rushed writing, but I wanted to get this out to you.

Please tell me if I am annoying or anything else!

Ti amiga Suzanne

Domingo 7 Junio 2015

Hey! Hola Roberto!

By the way you describe your meditation, it seems that you are a super master at visualisation. This is going to really help you with other types of meditation. You are truly capable of leaving your cell and generating a form of freedom for a while! This is incredible.

You have to explain to me about prison gangs. Do you have them on death row?

What you shared about the sensations when you get angry is fascinating. My body does something similar. it has real difficulties in coping with the energy of anger. My throat and lungs can't take it. When I am angry now, it is either super short or I have to turn it into a real constructive anger otherwise my throat and lungs simply turn weak.

P.S. I have noticed the endings of your letters: "always with love and respect". I am speechless. It feels grounded and grounding. Can't quite explain but thank you.

Lunes manana. I want to check with you what I experienced last night. During my sleep, I "landed" in your cell, then my cat followed me inside. You were unaware of me. Everything is pretty blurry and it completely threw me by surprise and repulsion to find myself in your cell in death row! Your arms caught my attention, the upper part of your arms, especially the left one. Do you have a birthmark or tattoo there? It was on the top front part of your left arm. It looked like a messy tattoo. I want to know if that was a dream or an astral travel or remote view. I could also not believe my cat flew right behind me and landed in your cell. You were playing cards or touching papers sitting on your bed. I was impressed by you because your energy is extremely strong and stubborn (in a good way). You felt powerfully anchored and grounded inside yourself like a mountain. Your body felt designed to be flexible and greatly starved for movement.

I freaked out by what was happening and to see my cat flying in there too. It shocked me. I was horrified at being inside death row.

I propelled myself out of your cell and landed in the corridor just outside your cell door. Still horrified at finding myself there, I ejected myself out and landed in some meadow by a river. From there, I went back into my sleep.

I feel vulnerable sharing this with you and am curious about what you are going to think about it. I am still quite shaken by it even now.

Until then, I am sending you a big hug.
Suzanne

June 21st 2015

Suzanne,

How are you feeling today? As for over here I am doing alright. It's always good to get your letter and sit on my bed to read it. It's my great escape.

I am good. There is still no news on my appeals and about when they will resume executions. But no news is good news. I read an article in a Time Magazine about "the last execution". It was detailing all that is wrong with the death penalty and how more people are changing their minds about it. It shows that the death penalty will be abolished, it's just a question of how long it'll take.

You should have seen me two days ago. If I could turn red I was red. I was listening to the radio, a song came on by Shakira called "Hips don't lie". I had gotten up to make a cup of Iced Tea and was dancing to the song (my Suzanne assignment!). I had turned my back for several minutes and when I turned around, a guard was standing at my door with a huge smile. I felt embarrassed but not too much. When my radio is on I cannot hear the door open because I have headphones on, but hey, it was fun and I was laughing after he left. :-)

Other than that things are pretty much the same over here. Tomorrow I'll go out to feed the birds and get some sun.

As for your "astral" visit here. I guess I can confirm that I am not easily shocked. I must admit that at first I was amazed. In all my years writing to my Swiss sister she had mentioned knowing people who can transport their life energy to other places. So I knew it exists. If I hadn't known that it is possible than yes, I would have been shocked. But after the first few moments of amazement, a funny thought came into my head and it was that I needed to learn how to do that. I think it was around that time I finished the work for the guy downstairs, so my bed would have been full of papers.

I may have been aware you were here but not know it was you. I have been seeing flashes from the corner of my eyes but by the time I look over nothing is there. The flashes happened more than once but I sometimes wonder if it's just my eyes playing tricks on me.

I honestly wish you were visible so you could sit on the bed and we could talk like normal people. And hey, if it doesn't take too much out of you, you are welcome here whenever you want to visit.

I do think you are right with how you saw me; my body is designed to be flexible and of late I have been doing stretches mostly because my back and hip are giving me problems and it helps a little to stretch. Yes, my left arm does have a tattoo, a gang tattoo from when I was on the streets. I was 18 years old and I got it at a party when I was high from a guy who was there. The weird thing is that it is covered with my shirt sleeve and I am only without a shirt when I shower or sleep. So you saw it nonetheless.

Thank you for sharing this experience with me. Like I said I don't mind you popping in, it will give me a chance to see what you look like since you haven't sent a photo of yourself.

Sharing Our Life Journeys

Con cariño y respect tu amigo.
Keep smiling
Robert

Thursday 11th June 2015

Hi Robert,

I walked to town again and I have to admit that it must even take me longer because all the roses are out. So, I stop a lot on the way. You can imagine me as a giant French bee who can't resist roses and who is getting her dose of rose perfume, for free, on the streets. The best ones I have found are yellow, they smell super-duper sweet: heaven on a stalk! :-)

I read a beautiful quote the other day, it went something like: "You do not need to find love. You just need to remember that you are already the vessel of love". Maybe you can send heart energy and love into your hip when you meditate. You could also do the Ho'oponopono prayer to your body and hip. It should help whilst you wait for medical progress.

Sometimes I also struggle with loving life. I can be full of frustrations: financial, professional, being single, health, issues with my landlady and so on. Sometimes I feel life is just a burden. In those moments, I remember that it is all a gigantic illusion because I am not a material being having a spiritual experience but the contrary: I am a spiritual being having a human experience. This perspective changes everything for me.

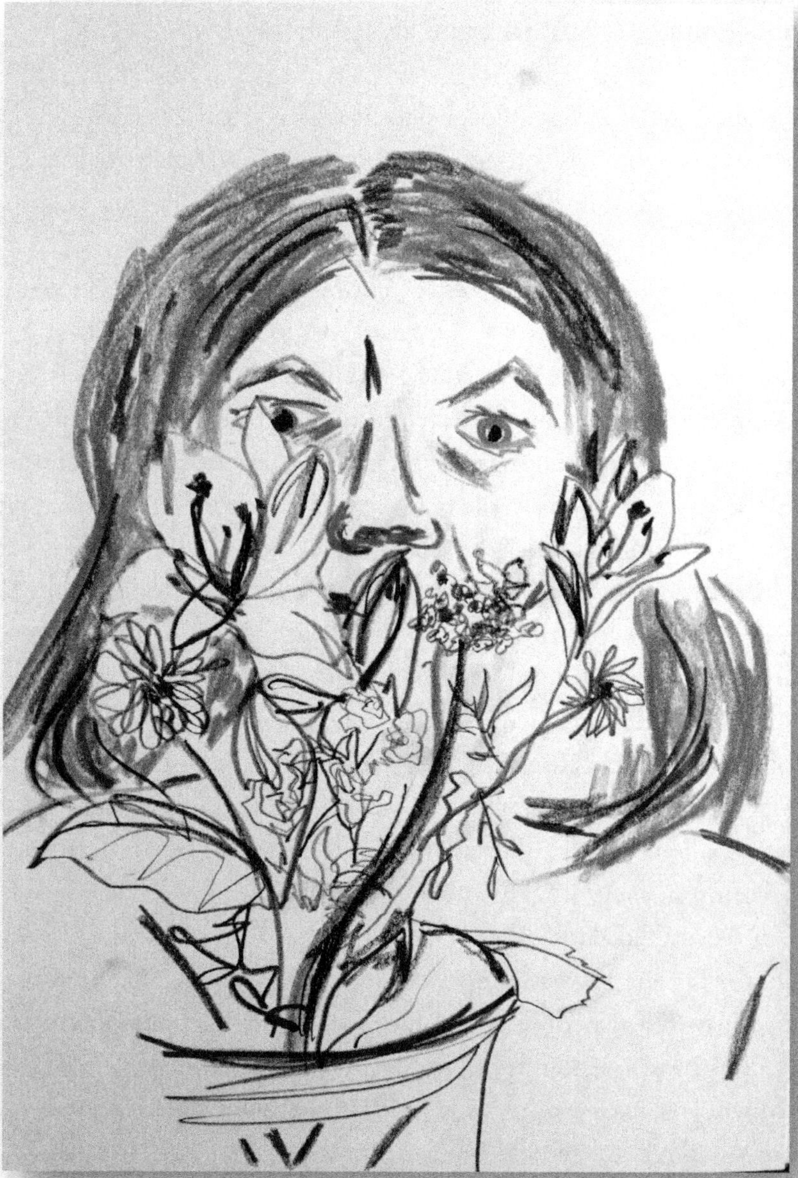

When I feel low, I also make sure to feel gratitude as usually a low is a lack of gratitude. Sometimes, I forget though, so stay in my low moods for too long! Every time without fail, when I reconnect with gratitude, I shift back into aliveness.

Guess what? I have never had handmade tortillas and I am glad to see that you have to do your dishes. Just finished doing the evening lot myself. I am sad to hear that you do love to cook and can't.

Have I fallen in love? Yes, of course! My late husband even if it ended up being a destructive relationship. In my twenties, I felt crazily in love with a guy studying conservation with me. I could even remember past lives we shared together. It was a truly beautiful love but I was still traumatised by my married life and somehow we drifted apart. In the last ten years or so, I have fallen in love mainly with guys who had little interest in me. Unrequited love does suck!

From time to time, I wonderfully fall in love with life. I love that feeling. I also love my dear friends with deep appreciation and caring. Although I do also struggle with friendships as I am quite a loner. I can definitely neglect my friendships! My friend Sam who is South African and his girlfriend Charlotte are part of my soul family. Sam can challenge me with his strong personality. In fact, we can both challenge each other but it feels that this is how we trigger an evolution in each other.

I feel a special love made out of deep appreciation for my current mentor Dr Joe Dispenza. He is a powerful human being creating a huge impact on people. I feel lucky to know him personally a tiny bit, as I have been able to share many hugs, embraces, chats with him when his workshops were small and intimate. He is actually very funny and playful. Wonderful qualities.

"To fall in love is easy but to remain in love is something truly special" is a quote on a magnet which lives on my fridge door. I bought that magnet years ago so that I could remain nourished by those words. I look at its image of an elderly couple gazing into each other's eyes with joy and appreciation for their life's journey together. It helps me as I have not fallen in love for many years.

Tell me more about those two girls you loved.

Thank you for sending me a hug. I have put my left hand on my heart to receive your energy hug.

I am sending you love.

Suzanne

Sabado 13 Juno 2015

Dear Robert,

So, Robert danced, Robert has danced, Robert laughed after he danced, Robert is the dancing King!

I celebrate your dancing whilst I am in the garden, in the shade. There is a lovely fresh breeze. In the background, I can hear urban cars, plane noises but also close by the sound of the wind in the trees and the occasional bird. I love the sound of trees in the wind.

Yesterday, we saw a teenage magpie in the garden with Scarlet. That teenage fellow had lost his youth plumage and did not bear yet his full black and white feathers. He or she, well, looked impressively ugly. We had such a laugh.

My favourite part of your letter is your dancing to "Hips don't Lie"! It is the first time ever in all your letters that you say something positive about a guard "with a huge smile" as you put it. This is incredible. That's the magical power of dance! And then you mention how fun it was and how you were laughing after the guard left. This is the first time you describe such freedom! I want to frame this letter.

I really get the sense of how macho your world is. Remember the story of Dr Len and how the prison closed after three or four years of him doing the Hawaiian traditional prayer to even the walls! Your dancing also spontaneously broke some of the macho vibes. I feel hope!

I see how hopeful you are for the abolition of the death penalty. This would be a massive step for you and many others but also in the general American psyche. I cannot imagine how it must feel to have your own execution as a future event. We are all going to die for sure but how makes a huge difference.

Let me tell you about energising your body and mediation with breath work. If you do the breathing before your Idaho "escape" or as part of any meditation, magic will start to happen to you even more. You will feel more energy and less matter. This is what I am going to be doing this summer in Germany with Dr Joe Dispenza. Through the breathing, we access other dimensions and higher levels of consciousness with no psychedelic drugs but by further activating our pineal gland. I can't wait!

By the way, it has been a month since I received a letter from you. I have not heard about your response to my idea of a book together.

Onto my little excursion flying in and out of your cell. I thought "oh shit" when you confirmed your left arm tattoo. It is amazing how calmly you took that story. A while back you said that nothing much will shock you. I can see that is true. I was afraid that you would freak out. I have no control over this kind of travel or extra sensory awareness. Let us hope we both progress in that kind of connection and can meet one day energetically.

My friend Roberto made a cheeky remark about the fact that I haven't sent you a photo of myself. I like when you tease me. :-) I feel that how I look is irrelevant to our connection, what matters is what we share.

It feels really good to be sharing again after a patchy month.
Signing off for now.
Suzanne

June 28th 2015

Suzanne,

Hey there! I received your letter over the weekend, and it is great to hear from you and know that you are well. Thank you so much for the poems and the story of the life of Hafiz. I've read the poems and they make me truly think about love. Thank you for telling me about the roses and I couldn't help myself, I had to laugh as I read you were a giant French bee that couldn't resist the roses.

It has been a bit stressful here. There haven't been any executions because there is a challenge to whether or not the drugs this State uses are constitutional. All death rows in America are different. We are expecting a decision this coming week so everyone is a bit on edge. Our lawyers say that it is unlikely that they'll vote in favor of us. But as soon as the ruling is handed down the prosecutor will be asking for warrants of executions.

There is a lot of speculation as to what will happen. I think they'll pick one person and execute him and if it goes without difficulties, they'll start up regularly. It is always good when there is a delay in executions but with the good often comes some bad. There were four people who have finished their appeals when the challenge with the drug happened. Now there are six people. We should know tomorrow what the decision is. After your appeals are exhausted you face execution.

Laura was 14 years old at the time of the murders. She is the mother of my daughter. She was charged and sentenced to 32 years in prison. Her conviction and sentence were overturned because US law states that anyone under 18 years old has to have a parent or lawyer present when they are questioned by the police. There wasn't either for her. It was in the court papers why her conviction sentence was overturned.

They wanted me and Jake, the other co-defendant to testify. I refused because she is the mother of my child and I couldn't send her to prison. I wanted my child to have at least one parent free. Jake wasn't credible without my testimony so they offered Laura eight and a half years in prison and she accepted. She could have refused if she had wanted but she could have been resentenced to 32 years again. Now she's out.

Jake is here in another cluster on the other side of the row. I have seen him and he has caused drama. He hasn't changed. I feel bad that he still wants to con people but I am in a better place in my life and cannot let my path go astray for someone not willing to change. He got the same sentence as me.

We were caught because when we ran away with Laura she got worried about Jake so she called collect a mutual friend but the police were already on our trail. They traced the call. We were in a homeless shelter. They checked and found us. We were only on the run for nine days. I couldn't be there for our daughter's birth. But I wanted to.

The way you deal with the thoughts that life can sometimes be a burden is amazing. I plan to definitely start to put this awareness in my head: I am a spiritual being having a human experience. I'll see how I feel.

About the two women I fell in love with, first was Sophie. I was 15 years old and she was my best friend for two years. We ended up taking our relationship to a new level. It is or was one of my biggest mistakes because we ended up getting into a fight over sex. She had been molested and I wanted to take things slowly but then she got tired of it. I lost a girlfriend but more importantly I lost a best friend. Last I heard of her she had two kids and was married.

The second was Eva. She was 25 years old and I was 18. She had a two-year-old son from a previous relationship. I met her through a friend, and we fell in love quickly. We'd make out and fool around but we were always interrupted before we could make love. We ended the relationship because we figured it wasn't meant to be. Two weeks before these crimes happened, I called her in Idaho and we were going to give it another try. I was supposed to get my last cheque from the restaurant I worked at but that wasn't going to happen until a week after the crimes.

I was one week away from going back to Idaho to try and start a new life.

I don't know what happened to her. Those are my big loves. Eva knows what happened to me. My trial lawyer and appeal lawyer have talked to her.

Let me close here for now. I'll write more later. Until the next letter take care of yourself and be safe.

Con cariño y respect. Robert

Saturday 4th July 2015

Hi Robert,

Went to bed around midnight yesterday with multiple thunderstorms going on. Scarlet came into my room to view the show. It was impressive. We could see three different sets of lightning, to the right, to the left and in the centre and hear three sets of thunder. Eventually, the one in front came above us and heavy rain broke with loud thundering. Scarlet said it was even better than TV.

I am feeling a bit like my head is cotton wool as I haven't slept enough. At 4.30am I was awake and completely energized so I came downstairs. Outside it was completely foggy and I went walking in the garden, barefoot on the yellow sundried grass, soaked with the rain from our thundering show.

My hours have increased in the shop to three and it is getting more physical but I like the job. The volunteers are cool, the customers are friendly and there is a good team spirit. My boss can still be challenging. There is a lack of space to take a break or eat your lunch. That's a problem too.

Monday afternoon. Still no letter from you. Is there a problem with the post? I need to re-write what I wrote yesterday as my cat has been sick on my papers including your letter. She is often sick at this time of the year as she loses so much fur due to the heat and swallows it when she cleans herself. I try to brush her but she hates it and attacks me, claws out!

Sunday evening.

This afternoon, I found out that the fridge stopped working for a while and the butter melted and dripped everywhere. A great mess that now needs to be cleaned. A full fat mess! Cleaning is not my favourite activity, but I like it when it is clean afterwards. It had to be done anyway.

I am running to catch the last post now.

Suzanne

July 12th 2015

Suzanne,

I hope you are doing well. I am doing good. Keeping busy and sane. Things here have calmed down. The supervising attorney for the federal public defender's office sent out a bunch of letters, one coming to me. It says that at least for the near future there won't be any executions because there is a case of federal court that is telling our Department of Corrections that they need to amend their lethal injection procedures. Until then the state has agreed not to ask for any warrants of executions. This is great news for a bunch of guys who have finished their appeal process.

You said you ran your first death cafe since November. Can you explain what goes on and how you run it.

Don't forget to smile.

Robert

24th July 2015. 10.30am

Hi Robert,

A summer's rain outside… I watched "Contact" again. That film is so cool and meaningful. I love that it is not about space travel but dimensional travel. I am glad you are into that level of awareness too. Have you heard of Interstellar which came out this Autumn? It is another far-reaching film about space/time, black holes and gravity. They actually made scientific discoveries whilst working on the scientific aspects of the film.

Right, Roberto, here we go. Buckle your seat belt, here comes Suzanne answering your last three letters.

The first one made me angry actually! Angry at the stupidity of men. Let me explain. Your interaction about not losing face and the bullying situations, Oh my God! It felt that you guys were acting like a bunch of immature teenagers. You are all on death row and some of you are still carrying this macho need to prove yourselves. Then it made me think about who creates war in the world: men and this made me even more angry! Who rules the world: men! So, yes I was angry at the general stupidity and domination of men! Then I calmed down, I stopped my judgments, meditated some and really felt compassion for you guys: caged men. I think that most of you have not had many chances to be nourished with love.

I felt sad about your two love stories. You have loved for such short times and you were so young. You have had little love experiences and then, off you were on death row. Sad!

Avec amour et respect… SMILING!! Suzanne x

July 16th 2015

Suzanne, my friend,

I am a little concerned about my letters not getting to you. I am going to start keeping track of incoming and outgoing letters. I know at times there are walkouts at the postal service between the States and Europe.

Things here have been pretty much the same. There has been some drama but nothing that concerns me. I just try to stay busy and out of trouble. Physically I am doing good. Unfortunately, I can't go outside as much as I want but I am able to move around in the cell without too much pain. So that is good.

Your lightning storm sounded amazing. I guess since in America it was Independence Day, nature didn't want you all over there to miss out on the light show. :-) Seriously, I know it had to be truly beautiful and powerful.

I do miss your words. I get your letters but when there is a delay, it's hard. I would like to be able to write to you directly, it would be quicker.

Hey, I miss you teasing me. :-)
Robert.

Tuesday 28th July 2015

Hi Robert,

About the death café: I have been running one for over a year and a half now. We meet monthly, usually on a Monday evening, in a café. For two hours strangers meet to talk about death. It might sound odd, but it is freeing to be able to break that taboo and be at ease with our stories, emotions, worries etc. Death cafe is an international movement. I advertise mine on the general website which covers Canada, UK, USA, Sweden, Norway, Australia and the like of Western countries. It is a free event and if people want to contribute which most do, they give a donation. I have been deeply moved by people's stories, their views, their journeys, their vulnerability. It is systematically interesting even fascinating but mostly movingly inspiring, disturbing at times, surprisingly funny even. I make sure nobody dominates the discussion and that no one is left out. Listening with respect is key.

This is not a tease but you are giving me the impression to be lazy spiritually recently. Am I right?

Take care, shake yourself spiritually, shake ya body, smile in your heart chakra, be kind to your back.

Suzanne :-)

July 23rd 2015

Hi Suzanne,

It does appear that the letter that was lost was the one regarding your offer to write a book with me. I hate that you didn't get this letter.

My answer like I said is of course I would be interested. I want people out there to see what we go through in here and what it means for us to have pen friendships. If society could see how people change in here, either religiously or like me spiritually, it would help. But it is hard to show society. For the most part the media only wants to show how bad we are. The only true outlet we have are the people we meet as pen pals.

Some inmates use the pen pal system as ways to make money. They take advantage of the kindhearted, asking for money and if someone doesn't send money then they quit writing. For them, it is a business and it often makes people stop writing to us in prison. However a lot of us are sincere about wanting to connect.

You are right about what you wrote regarding the death penalty being abolished one day and that this decision is also in our hands, us inmates rather than only politicians and pressure groups.

The macho world of prison is a harsh reality. In here, if you show weakness you tend to be treated as a victim. But if you stand up for yourself, others won't pick on you. But there is also the reality that trust is sacred. Even if you have someone you are close to, you can't fully trust them. It is just part of being in prison. You never know how and who will betray you. I have two people I trust and know won't betray me.

I had to laugh as I saw your adventure in the garden with the teenage magpie. It is amazing how the majority of bird species once hatched from their eggs are so ugly but as they grow to adulthood they become some of the most beautiful animals. It is crazy.

I am not in a prison gang. I would not qualify anyway because I have made questionable decisions early on in my prison life which won't make me acceptable to be in a gang. I don't let anyone tell me who I can talk to and who I can't like those people charged with sex murders. Also my closest person in here is black and being Mexican myself would be a big no-no. Also, I have a big mouth and don't take orders too well.

There are no real gangs on death row because we are so limited in our contact. Some like to think they are. There are two pods that are supposedly with righteous people, those who think they are in gangs, but it's mostly a joke.

I do want a picture of you one day, so I can see who I am writing to. But this is a choice you have to make. I am fine with how it is now. I just like to tease you about it from time to time. :)

SMILE !

Robert

August 1st 2015

Hello Suzanne!

Hey there! I hope all is well over there and that this letter finds you in good spirits.

I received your letter last night and it was great to hear from you and thank you so much for the rose fragrance you smeared on the paper. I'll have to find a way at preserving it so it'll last.

I have seen previews on TV of Interstellar. There is the possibility that we'll be able to see it. The prison is putting newer movies on the prison channel during weekends. So this gives me hope that maybe we'll get to see it.

I get your anger over some of our behaviors, bullying and macho stuff. I know it is childish and it can be stupid but unfortunately this is the reality of in here. I try to stay out of drama and this is also why I won't talk to any bullies. It can lead to a worse situation like money being extracted, we call this rent. Like you said, it is immature, egocentric but if a person is allowed to bully they get a big head, their ego grows and they believe that people will just bow down to them.

Men tend to destroy and this is something that must change. As I look into the future, I see women begin to rise. But the truth is in order for the world to work in unison men and women must rise together as equals. The journey towards that has begun. I only hope it is not too late.

I have tried Ho'oponopono a few times. It has calmed me. It helps me gain new perspectives when dealing with certain situations.

Laura is Jen's mom. Jen my daughter. When Laura was in prison, Jen was raised by Laura's mom. This was a mistake but one, no one, would find out about until Jen was 14 and living with her mom. She told her mom how she was treated like a maid and sexually abused by Laura's step father. She also told me in a letter. She had it rough and I feel awful because I wasn't there to protect her. I know my situation prevented me but even so the guilt is always there. This is why I tried to push Jen into meeting my side of the family: my mom, grandmother, cousins, brothers, nieces and nephews. It never worked but they are there whenever she decides to reach out to them, and she will be loved. I hope one day she does decide to reach out to them.

I have now come to the same conclusion as yours that I am a spiritual being having a human experience. It has opened my mind to many new experiences when I meditate and how I deal with my body.

Guess what? I was moved downstairs and I have spent three days cleaning and scrubbing this cell. It is amazing how some people can live in such dirty and nasty conditions. I guess some just don't have any self-worth. It is a nice cell now but my back and hip are sore because of all the movement I did. So I spent yesterday lying down trying to let my hip rest.

Your death cafe sounds really interesting. I don't think that it sounds strange to meet up to speak about death. Most of society is afraid of death, so the subject becomes taboo and even dark. But as you say, it is freeing to think about it. There should be more discussion on death and what happens during the dying process. In having those discussions, it makes us more aware of life. So when someone dies we can celebrate their life too and not just grieve.

As for my new lawyer, it is always a culture shock when you get a new lawyer but from her visit, she sounds smart and very dedicated but only time will tell how it goes.

You say I was in a phase of being lazy spiritually. I must admit I did have about one week and a half of being lazy in all things, even spiritually. I think it was mostly because I wasn't meditating. I did one of the techniques you showed me. The first time I did it, I held my breath and slowly released it but I only did it once. Later I reread your letter and realized that I needed to do it a lot more before I went into my usual meditation. When I did, instead of going to my falls, I went to a car crash when I was about eight years old. I freaked out. I didn't do it for about two weeks after that. Now, I am back to normal practice. I am doing the deeper breath only once a week. It helps me by taking me back through my past.

The stickers you added on your letter are fun and made me smile as I was reading your letter. The weather here has been hot but this new cell is actually cooler because my old one had the sun beating down on it so the wall absorbed the heat. This cell doesn't do that so it is a relief. But hey, if you want some of this heat you can have it. :-)

I dance a few times a day now. Sometimes, it is just for a few seconds, sometimes a few minutes. It all depends, but there are times that I'll dance and it looks like a spasm and it's fun. Thank you for turning me onto the new craze of dancing. I've realized how much it actually relieves stress.

Well, hey, let me close here, until the next letter, stay safe and keep smiling.

Robert

Saturday 22nd August 2015

Ola Roberto!

Como estas? So much to tell you. I thought of you a lot this week with your birthday and the anniversary (if we can call it that) of you entering the row—19 years now. I imagine this must have been a week of mixed feelings for you. I trust you spoke to your mum and your Swiss sister. :-)

Do you celebrate each other's birthday with your friends on the row? How did you celebrate yours?

I am moved and glad you are on board and your usual open-minded self about us writing a book together. You are going to have a voice in the world. Let us think how we can turn this daring, crazy idea into reality.

Update on the teenage magpie. He has been a regular in our garden and for a long time, he looked uglier and uglier. I thought that it had some plague type disease but, hey, slowly and surely his body started to grow those handsome deep black feathers that show a tinge of dark green and then his white feathers fell into place too. His head remained bold and ugly. Bless him or her! He is probably still around but looking like the others so I can't recognize him. During my walks, I had noticed other teenage ones with their bald necks and heads, semi grown feathers skipping their ugly steps. Now they are all grown-ups and playing good lookers.

You mentioned feeling odd when breathing deeply before the meditation. Indeed, the breathing will give you all sorts of strange reactions as it shifts your energy. It can be quite extreme like nausea all the way to a gentle tingling or feeling super energized. Just be open, don't judge, don't analyse, but feel, observe, be present with it. When you breathe with intention and awareness, memories might come back, shaking and spasms might be triggered. It is releasing trapped energy which is frozen in our bodies and cells, old emotional energy.

Onto my meditation retreat in Germany. We were 538 participants from around the world, in a vast and beautiful hall. I am not sure how to start telling you about what happened there and since. Simply put, my soul and spirit have been raw since having experienced such high frequency levels of love, energy and consciousness. I cried from seeing and feeling beings of other dimensions, landscapes of colours and light which are alive.

We learnt more about activating our heart energy and when over 500 people do that at the same time, you can imagine the intensity. We learnt to activate our pineal gland and did a four hour long meditation that felt like 30 minutes. Tears were running out of my eyes and nose from soulful bliss and the joy of coming home.

It is difficult to put in words, especially written ones.

My friend, I better stop here, until next letter, carry on dancing and keeping the birds happy.

Suzanne

September 1st 2015

Suzanne,

I haven't heard from you in a while and I am a little worried. It has been almost three weeks since I last received anything. The last thing I received was the birthday card you sent and I want to thank you for that.

Things here are the same. I have been trying to stay busy and out of trouble. The out of trouble part is difficult because of some recent events. But I have been able to stay away from it. I've been going again to the recreation pens but my hip then hurts and I am unfortunately immobile for the next day. But I think it's worth the trade off. It feels great to feel fresh air.

As for recent events, there have been a lot of moves lately. A guy was moved in here named Pablo and along with him came negative energy. I have been trying to keep my mouth shut. Two weeks ago Pablo and another guy attacked an old man who is 71 years old. Let me explain. We have what the prison calls a recreation team (rec team), these are the guards who take us out to the pens. They have tasers. They are a type of gun which sends 50,000 volts of electricity. It is not lethal but does incapacitate someone. On one of those going out moves, they took Pablo, the other guy and the old guy Joe. Our hands are cuffed behind our backs so one guy tripped Joe by kicking his legs and Pablo began kicking his body when he was down. Joe apparently got hurt before it could be stopped. Because of this attack we got Pablo on our pod now. I have had to hold my tongue because I know Joe and I like him. He is a bit crazy due to his age but it has angered me because to beat up an old man is off limits in prison rules. These rules are unwritten among us here. I hate the bully factor, the fact that it was two on one. And now that negative energy is around us. So far Pablo hasn't said anything to anyone so I am thankful because it has given me enough time to let my anger cool. Anyway enough with that.

The court that I am waiting on comes back from vacation either today or next Monday so hopefully in the next two weeks a decision will be handed down and I will at the very least know where I stand. I will let you know.

Until then, be safe, with care and respect.
Robert

September 7th 2015

Hello there,

Things here have been somewhat stressful. Today the new guy Pablo attempted to attack an inmate who was out cleaning the pod. He said that he would try to attack everyone in here whenever he gets a chance. He wants to be moved so this is his tactic to be moved. There isn't anything we can really do except wait and see what happens.

Also, things here have been somewhat tight financially. My mom hasn't been able to send any money the last two months, so I am using what my Swiss sister sends for phone time. My mum has had a few medical issues she has had to take care of that. It's been tight but I have been able to get the necessities and that is all that matters.

I have been going out to the recreation pens and it's good to get some fresh air especially the last few times because it rained. When it rains you can smell the freshness of the air, the oxygen around us is clean and you can feel the coolness of the air. But today when I went out there were swarms of mosquitoes so I was glad to come in. I did end up with a bunch of bites which are horrible because they itch and it's hard not to scratch.

The new cell is nice. It does feel different mostly because the table, stool, toilet and sink are arranged on the opposite side.

Just finished reading the papers you sent about the life and work of the poet Hafiz. First I am absolutely amazed at how he was able to find Perfection. His two 40 day vigils had to take extreme discipline and each time he began the vigil he held one thought or desire only to come out of it with a different outlook on life and his path.

Secondly, the paper made me rethink my thoughts on the Creator and God. I've always known there was a higher power but now as I contemplate on what was written I have realized that I want to embrace God. I can do this through and by love. I don't have to concentrate on the bible or a church or Christianity. I don't like organized religions but the true essence of God is love and to show reverence and honor God I must and accept love for what it is.

Also I understand why you say dance is important. It is a way to relieve stress but also a way to spread love. Like when I first started and I got caught by the guard and he laughed and I laughed! I hadn't realized that throughout my letters to you I hadn't said anything positive about the guards until that point. It was interesting that it came through me dancing!

I took some time to reflect on my approach to many things, for example Pablo who beat up the old man. Since he got here I have tried to find a way to get him moved out but now I know I need to leave it alone and concentrate on the people I talk to and with what is positive.

Thank you Suzanne. I don't think you can imagine how Hafiz's life has impacted me the way it did. I must say it has made me re-examine a lot of things.

Well, let me close here. I'll write a little more later. Right now I want to meditate and re-read the paper so until later, smile. Robert

September 14th 2015

Hello again!

Sorry I stopped writing yesterday. The guards came in to do cell searches which I absolutely hate. Up to eight guards come into the pod and we have to line our boxes against a wall. Then two guards will stand at my cell door and ask for my boxers, t-shirt and shower shoes. So, I have to get naked in front of them. They search the clothes and ask me to lift my arms, open my mouth, turn around, bend over, spread my butt cheeks, lift each foot. Then I can get dressed. I am handcuffed and put outside my cell while two guards enter my cell, check the boxes for items we aren't allowed to have, check our beds, often unmaking them. Once they are done, I am allowed to come back in. If they take something they must give us a contraband receipt. For the most part the guards are respectful. This routine happens once every three months, unless there is an issue.

So that meant about two hours of putting my cell back in order, then washing the floor and seeing if anything was taken. Luckily nothing was.

Before I went to sleep last night I did a little meditation and wanted to think of ways I could take myself out of my comfort zone. I'll still stick with exercising but also I realized that I sit on my bed too much and because it is somewhat soft, I do tend to recline on it. It can lead to laziness and cause discomfort to my lower back. So I am going to start sitting on my box a lot more and this will force me to sit up straight. We'll see how that works out.

I have been doing the Hawaiian prayer a lot and have it now hanging by my mirror. When I get up to wash my face or hands or even just to make a cup of coffee I say it. The first two times were without incident because I said it in my head. The third time, I said it out loud, my neighbor was at the front of his cell when I said "I love you, I am sorry, please forgive me, thank you". I guess he caught the thank you and he asked "for what?". I just had to explain that I was doing a prayer and it was part of it. He said "OK" and went back to doing whatever he was doing. I like how I have it set up because I just look into the mirror, say the prayer and move to my next task. It is nice and it puts me in a good energy.

I have another pen friend and she is from the UK too. She got my name from Human Writes, another anti-death penalty organization in England. There isn't much of a connection between us though.

Other than that things are the same. Still dancing and have been caught a few times, got some smiles and odd looks by the guards, they think I'm losing my mind but that's OK. :-)

Today is interesting, I am fasting. I am writing and my stomach is grumbling but I want to persevere to help clean my system so I can properly focus on my pledge.

Anyway, I want to get this out to you so let me close here for now. I hope all is well out there. Until then take care of yourself and be safe. I am sending energy and love your way and hey, don't forget to smile.

Always with love, honor and respect,

Robert

> **I love you**
> **I am sorry**
> **Please forgive me**
> **Thank you**

Hello Suzanne,

Hey there! Just wanted to send you a card to say hi and to thank you for this wonderful prayer and for all the help that you have given me. You have taught me a lot and I am so greatful that you came into my life.

You are an amazing woman who has shown me love and respect and for that I will forever be thankful and greatful. Thank you above all for showing me kindness and for seeing Robert for Robert.

Por un mujer que es bella in alma y en persona. Gracias mi amiga.

With my love, respect gratitude and appreciation Always,

Robert

Sharing Our Life Journeys

My pledge of non-violence.

My pledge and vow of non-violence
is a pledge I have taken after I realized
how much energy I was wasting on anger
and hatred that went into violence.

I wanted to no longer hurt other people
as this is how I dealt with emotions.
In order for me to better myself,
I have had to let go of rage, anger and hatred.

In not being violent anymore
I am to finally deal with those emotions and in dealing with them,
I in turn, learn who I truly am.

It is a pledge that I hold dear
because it is a standard I have set for myself.
To break it not only affects me but harms others.

Maintaining this pledge
allows me to open my heart and mind
to love, knowledge and positive energy.

Only then can I truly make a positive difference in my life
and the life of those around me.

Wednesday 4th November 2015

Good morning Robert,

Trees have lost more or less all their leaves and, in some areas, it is like walking on a golden path.

For nearly two full days and one night, we were under the London fog, thick fog that lingers and brings humidity and blocks light off. I don't really like it, it makes me feel claustrophobic!

I am going to burn your vow of nonviolence today as it is now beautiful out and it will be good to give it to Father Sun and Mother Sky. Thank you for entrusting me with this task.

Sunday, we did a worldwide coherence meditation with Joe. He gave a scientific teaching on heart coherence and then everybody joined to meditate together for peace and healing the planet. Studies have shown that when large groups of people meditate at the same time there is a reduction in crime.

The meditation was very simple and beautiful. After a while I started to feel I was a cell of Gaia (Mother Earth) and I was receiving and giving so much energy that I started to have pins and needles in my entire body. I was passing this intense energy to animals, birds, the ice of Arctic and Antarctica, to polar bears, the soil (a lot of healing there), to humanity. It was very intense and powerful. I am still feeling the effects and still have pins and needles moving around my body. By the end, I felt deeply healed, moved and I had strong feelings of hope, love, connection. Went to bed and had the most peaceful sleep with the most graphic dream where fear was literally removed out of all my blood vessels!

I will tell you when there is another meditation like that you can join us in your own way.

OK, mi amigo con los angeles Smile Suzanne x

PS. I faced the sun, made my intention to release your pledge to the sun, sky, universe so that it becomes one with life force. I also thanked you and your life for your trust. Then I crunched the paper and set fire to it. I watched it burn motionless.

October 8th 2015

Hey there!

Received your letter last night and was glad to hear from you and to know all is well over there.

A woman in Georgia has been executed. Then another state puts executions on hold because they can't get the execution drugs and this last week, we found out that our state tried to import the lethal injection drugs from India and got caught. The US customs found out and held up the cargo. It was illegal. At last count six people here are done with their appeals. So hopefully it will take a long time to get the drug protocol fixed because once they start they'll go full out and I know four of the six who will be executed. That always makes it harder.

I have been reflecting on who you are to me.

First and foremost you are a friend. A word whose meaning I do not take lightly. When I call someone a friend I mean it. Second, you are a teacher. You have taught me a lot about the spiritual world, meditation and about myself. Since I have known you I discovered more about myself. But ultimately when looking at that question of who you are to me, I best answer it by saying you are someone I care a lot about, someone who has shown me the deeper meaning of love and has taught me there are many ways to love. You are someone I respect with all my heart and you are someone I will take with me in my next life. Thank you Suzanne for being a friend, a teacher and someone who sees me as a person.

Robert

Tuesday 10th November 2015

Dear Robert,

I am excited to share this with you: I have just gained some deeper understanding on how to activate the Hawaiian prayer and how it works. I have been listening to a meditation guided by Dr Hew Len. It is about the "mother/child" relationship. What he means really is about the conscious and unconscious mind, the first being the mother and the latter the child. It makes sense as all our childhood memories which we don't necessarily remember are stored in our unconscious mind. In short, lots of stuff: traumas, stress, unresolved issues are stored at the level of the child.

So, you recite the ho'oponopono literally to your unconscious mind, to the child inside of you. In a way, you are acknowledging your oneness to all of your life and asking for forgiveness for all the pains there has been, and saying I love you to your inner child. It is powerfully healing. Please give it a try.

I read your last letter on a bus. I normally can't read in buses, but I read it solidly in one go. I am so relieved that you received my two books. Ordering them was not an easy process and I wasn't sure you would get them. I am in the process of reading the one of lucid dreaming by Charlie Morley. Wayne Dyer was a truly amazing man.

He died at the end of August, age 76. I know you will love his book. He is one of the most influential spiritual teachers of our time.

Before I go, I have some difficult questions to ask you. They have been on my mind. Could you be executed just like that, I mean in the space of a few days? Could it happen without me knowing?

As part of my lady's cycle those last few days, I have felt sadness, bereavement and feared your death—the loss of our friendship. I was afraid that you could be executed at any point without any warning. Thanks for answering those painful, delicate but much needed questions.

OK! More soon with love
Suzanne

November 12th 2015

Hello Suzanne,

Just a quick letter to update you on my legal visit today. I met the lawyer taking over my case, another woman. She seems pretty nice and shows interest in wanting to help. I was taken to a type of cell at the visitation area and my handcuffs were taken off. My lawyer came in a different room across from me and we were separated by a sheet of glass. We could talk as there were holes on the side and we could see each other. The visit was for an hour and there was a guard outside the room on my lawyer side. He couldn't hear what was said and he didn't watch us. She has handled capital cases or death penalty cases for 15 years. Unlike when my previous female lawyer first visited, she was full of questions about my family, my past and she showed a genuine interest in getting to know me. I'll also have another lawyer, a man, but I didn't get his full name spelled out. I am not sure of his name. But I will meet him sometime soon. It looks like I'll have a good legal team, but we'll have to wait and see how it goes. I am crossing my fingers that it will be good.

I just want to send you a quick letter but I think I will send it off next week when I write to you. So I can save a stamp. I hope you don't mind. Until then I'll be sending good thoughts and positive energy your way.

With love,
Robert.

November 17th 2015

Hey there!

Good morning. Received your letter last night and it is always good to hear from you and to know that you are well.

Things here have been alright for the most part. I continue to be tested on my anger and non-violence resolve but I have been able to keep my mind straight. A new development for me is that while talking in here I often use profanity. I know you can't tell through letters because when writing it is easy not to use it but in talking one day recently I realised how much swearing I was using. I have now taken an active decision to control the way I talk. It will take some time and I find myself catching words as I am saying them. My goal is to get to a point where I can have conversations without having to use profanity.

My test of non-violence happened with a guard. It was more about controlling my anger. I have had an issue with this guard before. Once I went to the recreation pens and because there were swarms of mosquitoes I requested to come in after five minutes. He didn't want to bring me in but another guard did, so his ego was hurt. On Monday, I told him I wanted to go out but when they did start pulling people out, I was skipped. I got mad and went to the shower instead.

That same guard came to put me back in my cell. He kept my door open to try to intimidate me and he tried to start an argument. In the past I would have engaged into the argument but I realised what was happening so instead I turned my back to him and backed up. When he saw I wasn't going to engage with him, he shut the door and took the handcuffs off. After he left I began to smile because I was thinking how proud I was of myself. Anyway, it was an eye opening moment for me of how much progress I've made but also a realisation of how much more I need to do because honestly I shouldn't have even said anything to begin with.

You mentioned participating in a global heart coherence meditation with Joe Dispenza. It sounded like a great experience. Do you have stuff on global peace meditations as I would like to learn more on that. If it happens again, let me know of the time and I will join in.

As for Gaia, I have heard the name but I didn't put it together with the sacred name of our planet Earth. I am sure I had learnt it was the name used by the Greeks for Earth but I didn't remember until you wrote about it.

Sometime soon, I am going to send you a few letters. They will have in my own words what happened during the killings, my legal psychological profile at the time of entering death row and my legal confession in another. I need to wait for my legal box to get brought from property so I can dig out the paperwork. Property is a place in the prison unit. Store bought items such as appliances, clothing or shoes go to property first to be inspected and for our inmate prison numbers put on them. Property also is a storage area for legal boxes with our legal paperwork in them.

As for our book, I do talk about it to some of the others and I often say, "me and my friend from England are putting a book together".

Well, hey, let me close here. I am getting old and need to take a nap. :-)

I'll write more over the weekend so until then take care of yourself, be safe and dance, dance, dance. You and Scarlet are in my thoughts and I send energy, love and positive thoughts your way.

With love, joy and happiness and smiles.

Robert

November 22nd 2015

Hello Suzanne,

Hey there! It is great to hear from you and to know that things are good and that you are doing well.

I have been doing the same old thing: trying to stay busy.

For a while, I had thought of writing a book and it was a fictional romance (well you know me!) but I could never get motivated. But when you suggested your idea, I was really excited and still am. It will give the outside world a view of what truly happens in a friendship between a person out there and a person in here. Also, I hope that it will open some eyes to the spirituality of love and what positive effects it can have on the world and people. I agree to add our letters and in fact I want everything about my life in the book.

I am anxious to get the parts of the book you have done so far. I truly believe that it is a great idea so let's get going. When I receive it, I will take a few days reading and rereading it, taking notes and then I'll sit down and write to you.

I am curious to how you look. Your trip to the hairdresser has only raised my curiosity because I wonder what colour your hair is. Haircuts here are done by us. Typically, a person either grows their hair or keeps it short. A few people use a comb with their electric razor or the beard trimmers the guards loan out. I grow my hair for about a month or two then get the beard trimmers and cut it real short then I use the electric razor to shave it bald. It is just easier and less maintenance. I used to be able to keep it constantly bald when we were allowed to use manual razors. Then I didn't have to buy shampoo.

Keep smiling, stay safe and dance.
Robert

December 29th 2015

Hi there,

I received your letter, and it was really good to hear from you and to know all is well over there.

I have started writing for the first part of our book. I have also found my legal confession at the time of my arrest after the murders, it was in a box at property. I went through it and reread what happened the night of the killings. It is 20 pages long. I honestly say that it was hard to go through it. As I read it, I realized how unemotional I was during the interview, but I remembered the feelings of that night.

As the first killing began, I remember the panic I felt as I realised that it had started and how after the first murder the panic turned to numbness.

I remained numb until my daughter was born nine months after we were arrested. I didn't find out until the day after when a guard came to me and told me that Laura had given birth. I had only seen Laura a few times after our arrest but never talked to her.

I was in such a bad place in my life. I didn't care what happened to me. But the day Jen was born, my life changed. It woke me up to what I had done. I hated myself for a long time after that. It is amazing how the birth of a child can make you reflect. I felt the guilt of taking three lives, the pain I put their families through, then the realization I would not be able to watch my little girl grow up. Then the pain I caused to my own family.

Not until 2004, did I start to deal with a lot of my past. As you have seen I still have my insecurities. I feel there is nothing I can do to take away the bad karma created by the killings. It will follow me to my next life. Not until this year, thanks to meeting you, have I been able to better understand my evolution. I am now clearer at focusing my energy into knowledge, love and meditation.

I still don't have an idea on how my new lawyer wants to proceed with my appeal. It was only her first visit and it usually takes a few to see or get an idea of what she will do, so far she wasn't able to read my file.

For the appeal and the possibility of a life sentence, there are many factors. Right now I am waiting on another person's case to be decided by the court. If the court rules it in its favour, the state will appeal. This could take up to six months or a year. If the US supreme court upholds the lower court's ruling, it will mean that 14 people along with that guy will have the possibility to have their death sentences overturned. I am one of them.

We will all have to go back to our trial courts and be resentenced. About two thirds of those cases will end up back on death row, just starting over the appeal process. There are many factors that would lead to me being resentenced to death.

My case led to a lot of career making moves. My trial lawyer and the prosecution attorney are now judges. My case was a high profile one, it got a lot of publicity so going back will put pressure on the state to resentence me to death. If there was only one murder there would be a possibility of a life sentence but with three, it doesn't look good for any prosecutors career to not seek a death sentence. Those are the reasons I will likely be put back on death row. There is a small chance though. The climate here and in America is changing regarding the death penalty. A jury consisting of 12 people have to unanimously sentence me to death. If one person says no and is able to hold that decision a mistrial will be given. The state will have another chance with a different jury to seek again the death sentence. If the verdict is not unanimous, I will be sentenced to 25 years for each murder, that's 75 years plus the 25 years for the conspiracy to commit murder and 10 and a half for armed robbery. 110 and a half years is basically natural life. But who knows? I am not the same person I was 20 years ago so that will be factored into any defence for a life sentence.

About my change in language (no profanity), it has been hard to change. I get into a deep discussion and before I realise it, I will have used profanity throughout it. But I am trying to be more conscious of how I talk.

Well hey, I see I've written a lot so let me close here so I can get this ready to go out. I hope all is well over there and that Scarlet is good. I'll write more later and hope to hear from you soon. Until then, take care of yourself and be safe. I am sending thoughts and positive energy your way and don't forget to dance and smile. :-)

Dance, Dance, Dance.

With my love, always, tu amigo siempre.

Robert

Wednesday 23rd December 2015

Dear Robert,

Thank you for sharing your feelings about the book. I have been feeling overwhelmed with the dimension of our project and its potential power.

I am amazed at your practice of reciting Ho'oponopono whilst looking into your eyes. I have not done that. I will give it a try. It feels that it could be powerful, difficult and beautiful.

You mention feeling numb after the first murder. This is the first time you share an emotion about what happened.

How does that feel for you? Feels like we are removing our masks, hey! We are both hitting the power of feeling vulnerable by going deeper into revealing who we are. I like your phrase: "I honestly say it was hard to go through the confession". It feels raw.

An important point you write about are your insecurities about the bad karma you have created by killing three people. As I was a practicing Buddhist for 19 years, I can assure you that, yes, you can change and transmute bad karma. I believe we all, through the numerous incarnations we have had, did awful and painful things which created what we call "bad" karma. For my part, I have been a Roman gladiator and a Japanese samurai around the eleventh century. I have been a warrior in past lives! I sometimes feel this is one of the reasons why in this lifetime I have been weak physically and experienced much pain in my body. It is my karmic retribution. Paying back some of the pain I had inflicted onto others. The key is our attitude each moment of our lives. I also remember being a maid in an English inn in the sixteenth century and an Amerindian woman. This is how much I remember of my past lives, for the time being.

You have killed, and this is a terrible thing. It has generated much pain for many and for yourself. Since then, you have evolved, understood, shifted emotionally and spiritually into heart energy, forgiveness and nonviolence. I believe this lessens your karmic creation.

By the time you die, I believe your karmic debt will be already reduced compared to if you had remained living with hatred, blame and self-disgust.

I would like to suggest that you meditate on self-love. Love and self-love will carry you to change even deeper your karma.

Maybe, there is another spiritual dimension to your murders. You six souls (the three killed and the three perpetrators) chose the killing before you all incarnated. At the soul level, you all needed, due to karmic reasons, this experience for your respective evolution. At this level of consciousness, you were all equal co-creators and there are no victims, no perpetrators as such. It is only my opinion, but in a way, it puts the responsibility back onto every single person involved. This by no means reduces the basic human level of suffering of your acts. In life, different levels are always simultaneously at play. For example, there is your level of beingness and awareness of what you do in your daily life and simultaneously the levels of beingness and awareness of your cells which is radically and utterly completely different from your daily life one. One cannot exist without the other.

How do you relate to this?

My hand is hurting, I have been writing solidly for over an hour and I need to massage it! Smile! Compassion dance for my hand! :-)

I had mixed feelings about reading your official psychological summary, but I did find the courage to read it. Thank you for sending it to me. The full 20 pages! I found it highly disturbing. I want to thank you for your trust and openness. This is strong stuff Robert. I cannot believe how much you have evolved. You must have had to go through some severe drug and alcohol withdrawal symptoms when you arrived on the row or after your arrest.

Now I have read this description of you age 18, I honour even more when you say that the word "friend" has deep meanings for you. You have birthed a new you since you started to change. I am more than impressed.

I read in it that you have Apache blood. I did not know that. It makes sense now how you naturally carry such powerful inner wisdom. You are of indigenous descendance. Respect to your Apache blood.

When I was in Arizona on a Dr Joe Dispenza workshop, before a meditation, I was just entering into a meditative state when I saw three elderly Amerindians people from a distant past. They came one at a time, close to my face, looked at me, super intentionally, deeply, right through into my soul and faded back into the dimension they came from. It was awesome and heart breaking as I wanted them to stay longer so I could interact with them, see them for longer.

I saw each one of them super clearly. I perceived their wrinkles, ancient wisdom, depth of perception. I felt the intensity of their purposeful visit. I had no control over them, I was in their hands. They were checking me out. They decided how long they stayed. This is one of my most precious moments of my life.

I have several Amerindian connections. I have felt them since being a little girl.

I am glad my photo adds a presence into your cell! I think I was afraid of your chronic falling in love. I felt vulnerable sending you my photo, but finally I have revealed a layer of myself I could not keep hiding any longer. But now it feels good and right and I am glad to be a visual presence for you.

I have just been listening to a radio program on the man who founded Lifelines and his pen friend is now on his death watch and within two weeks of execution. I hope you never have to go through that. There was the recording of a phone conversation between the two and the man sounds so calm, sane, loving, both resigned and wise whilst counting his last days of life. It was deeply moving and upsetting. This system of execution feels perverse. Like you, he felt he had evolved sufficiently to be able to view his life and execution from a greater perspective and wisdom.

Phew, that was quite a bit of catching up and writing.

Big smile. Suzanne

February 23rd 2016

Hey there Suzanne!

How are you doing? As for over here, I am doing alright. I just want to write a quick letter to let you know I have been moved again and I want to give you my my new cell number. I made sure that the guards would redirect all my mail to the new cell if need be.

So far it is a decent pod. I know a few people and have already lived close to four of them before. Changing cells is hard so I am glad I could. I haven't lived in this pod before.

When we move we are told to pack our property up. We are handcuffed and the guards take our property, put it on a tcart and roll it over to the new pod. They put our belongings in the new cell. Then they close the door and take the handcuffs off.

It is going to allow me to go to new recreation pens and talk to Eddie. That will be great to be able to catch up with him. It will be nearly four years since we have seen each other or spoken!

The cell itself was a complete mess. I guess the guy in here before had mental issues, one being paranoia. He is now in my old cell: 3G43. He thought that the prison was pumping poisonous gas through every crack in the cell walls. As a remedy he decided to fill in every crack with peanut butter and toothpaste. There are a few people who have lost parts of their mind in here. I know of six I think who have become crazy.

So, I got in here at about 9.45am and was able to get the guards to give me a mop, bucket and broom and I spent the next three hours or more, scrubbing the walls. Unfortunately, I am too short to do the ceiling so that will stay that way but for the most part the cell is as clean as I can get it.

I was upset to hear that you didn't get my birthday card to you with my drawing. I'll draw a new one and send it.

After reading Dreams of Awakening of Charlie Morley I found myself knowing I am dreaming whilst I am in a dream!

Well, hey Suzanne, I guess I better quit for now. I'll write more later. Until then please take care of yourself and be safe. Know that I am thinking of you and sending positive energy your way. Don't forget to smile. Con amor y con un sonrisa siempre. Robert

Wednesday 24th February 2016

Hi Roberto mi amigo de USA,

Today there was a fierce battle between the forces of winter and spring. This morning the roofs were white, the grass crispy with frost and now, in the sun it is like spring. I've just discovered, a South facing cafe which is within walking distance. I spent over an hour there this morning imagining I was in Italy whilst soaking in some winter sun heat, energy and Vitamin D.

I walked past the yellow rose bushes. They have been trimmed and are dormant. They made me think of you. :-)

Then I had a coup de foudre. A falling instantly in love and reciprocal. After the rose bushes, I fell nose to nose with a tiny, old dog, a Jack Russell, all slow in his age. It was an instant love affair on both sides. That made me so happy and nourished. This little doggy was just giving me so much love. A happy Suzanne.

Sunday. A little drained, peaceful, empty (nice empty) Suzanne here.

After reading an article on the menopause this morning (you didn't expect to be dealing with female hormonal issues when agreeing to have a pen friend. Smile!) I am understanding better what is going on with me. It is adrenal fatigue linked to hormonal changes and it all seems normal for my age. So this is quite a relief.

Yesterday evening I had friends over to celebrate my birthday and I felt so drained that I couldn't cope with preparing food so they did it. They seemed to enjoy it. I felt pathetic.

Today I am tired and in need for "nothing". Scarlet is out babysitting. She was really good and helped with dishes and cleaning up after last night (more than I could do).

I have three bouquets of flowers in the lounge from my party and I love it. The day I have more money, I want to have lots of flowers in my house. It really makes a difference. It nourishes my soul. They feel alive, vibrant, and are so beautiful.

That's it; I have gone all flat and empty now. I need to do some chi gong and yoga to move some energy.

OK, "this is it" as Michael Jackson said. Do you like his music? I do. We both do with Scarlet.

On this note, much love, apologies for only a tiny letter. That's the way it is.

Suzanne :-)

March 28th 2016

Hello there,

Just a quick note so I can send you the letter I wrote to my stepfather Jon. I want you to burn it to release my words to him. Thank you.

Nothing new here, I'll probably spend the next two days redoing your birthday card. Just wanting to let you know you are in my thoughts always and I hope all is well over there. So until I hear from you take care and be safe. And hey, don't forget to smile.

My letter to Jon:

Hello Jon,

I wanted to write to you this letter to let you know how much your brief time in my life meant to me. And to say thank you.

You weren't with us for long, about two years and a half. The time you spent with us I hold precious and though your leaving left a void that I didn't know how to deal with, I know that you left a positive path in all the lives you touched.

Thank you for being a part of my life and for always treating me and my brothers as your children. Before you came I never knew what it felt to have a father, but from the beginning you opened your arms and your heart to me.

You showed me what a man is supposed to be and throughout it all, you showed me that though blood is thicker than water that sometimes it isn't blood that bonds a son to a father. Your leaving left a void in my life. I did use that as part of my defense mechanism to avoid being hurt again. For that I am sorry that your memory was misused.

I hope that if you are in your next life or still waiting for your next life to begin that you'll be proud of the Robert I have become in the last eight to nine years.

I want you to know that I love you. I will forever treasure our moments like fishing, walking or just talking together. Your kindness, your love and your heart has left a lasting imprint on my life.

I pray that wherever you are that you are happy and that you are bringing the same love and joy to other lives.

Be safe Jon and may your energy spread throughout the world.

Always in my heart and memories.

Robert

Thursday 10th March 2016

Dear Roberto/a!

Roberta feels nice too, it brings a high tone to your name and frequency: carefree happiness. Maybe you can try to tune into Roberta when dancing and tame your inner feminine side! I am curious to your reaction to this spontaneous suggestion. Smile mi amigo/a!

Why on earth am I telling you this when in fact I needed to tell you something completely different. Something I have felt I need to tell you for quite a while.

I want to explain that I do not view myself as a spiritual teacher or mentor to you. I view myself as your spiritual companion and you are my spiritual companion in perfect balance.

I have never expressed this to anyone before, nor felt it like that. An on-going, slow moving, slow motion stream of consciousness is flowing between us for over a year now. I realise that I have certain knowledge which I share with you because you don't have much access to. Does that make sense? But that's it.

What you give me is the spiritual strength of what you go through in your daily life. And I thank you for this.

In kindness,
Suzanne

March 19th 2016

Hey there!

How has everything over there been going? As for over here things have been the same, just trying to stay busy and out of trouble. A busy mind is a sane mind. I received your letter and I wanted to meditate on your beautiful words.

I first want to say thank you for saying what you said. I do understand and I am truly amazed at how huge your heart is. To say I am your spiritual companion in absolute balance is truly an honour and privilege. I want to say that I feel the same way.

I truly believe that our fates are connected and that we met in past lives and that in future lives we will meet again. Who knows, maybe next time I'll be older than you and you younger. I have to say that reading what you wrote brought tears to my eyes.

I understand that it is hard for you to acknowledge and come to terms with the realization that you are in a way a spiritual teacher or mentor to me. However as we have agreed radical honesty is always first, I must be radically honest now. I understand your resistance to wanting to be a teacher or mentor, it is a huge responsibility and I can accept that you aren't my spiritual teacher or mentor but to some degree you are.

You have learnt from my journey growing up to where I am now spiritually. So we are teaching each other and in that process we are more companions than teachers but still.

Let me explain my views. In our journeys whether we are alone or with others, we must all become teachers. Ideally, we spend our lives gaining knowledge and connecting with the energy and love around us to better ourselves. But if we are truly bettering ourselves then we must also show others. We must share the knowledge we gain with others. Hence we must all become teachers.

To teach, to some degree is part of our journey and I understand your initial reluctance.

The reality is Suzanne, my sweet loving friend, that by writing our book, by sharing our experiences we are teachers.

We are sharing our knowledge with those wanting to read it and who are open to receiving it. We are spreading our love and energy into the world. Yes, you have taught me a lot.

Remember, before I met you, I believed I was prepared to move onto my next life. Now I know I wasn't even close to being ready. Thanks to you I am learning and in the process of co-authoring a book which will spread the love and compassion of a woman who is free and of a death row prisoner. We will show the world we can all change and learn.

Look Suzanne, I never expected to connect with anyone. I spent my life looking for a romantic love to fill the void I had growing up. Through all my rage and anger I wanted to be loved. But I have learnt that no matter how much someone loved me, until I accepted and loved myself, I could never fill the void inside myself.

I have connected with you. It's not the love I am so easily lured into but it is a type of love that is spiritual. The more I get to know you, the more I get to know myself. And I must be honest, in the beginning it scared me and sometimes it still does.

When I read how you view yourself as my spiritual companion I realized that it is love I feel. A different feeling but a more fulfilling one. I hope I haven't scared you off . :-)

You are special and I am grateful that you have come into my life and have taught me above else that I must love myself.

I have seen my friend Eddie on our way to the recreational pens. We tried to shake hands but it has been so long, we both felt awkward and we didn't know how to anymore. But it was great to catch up and see him.

    Well Suzanne, I better close here for now so I can get this ready to go out. I'll write more later so until then please take care of yourself and be safe and don't forget to smile.

    Con amor y con allegria (happiness) Robert.

Tuesday 29th March 2016

    Hola mi amigo,

    This is going to be a letter full of big news!
    I am writing in the sun. It has been alternating between sun and hailstorms for the last few days. A typical March weather for us.
    I was deeply moved reading about your re-connection with your friend. After more than four years! It seems unimaginable as you live in the same building!
    I realized how you live your life daily with this constant reality of court cases and how your future will be. I cannot possibly imagine how you cope with that constant tension and unknown. An unknown with only two options: execution or life imprisonment.
    So happy you could feel the heat of the sun in your cage. Thanks for saying you were a "bit envious" of me in that south facing cafe. You are always so polite and contained. You could have felt raging jealousy, but no, you were "a bit envious".
    Onto the big news. Number one: my health is really improving. I have more consistent energy. :-)
    Number Two: (extra big news) YO SOY IN AMOR!!! I have fallen in love!

It started at my birthday party (remember?) when my girlfriends, whilst they were busy doing the party cooking, ganged on me to go online dating. I have always had a big "No" to go online dating but for some reason I felt a vibrant "Yes". Maybe it is because I have turned 51 and have been single for many years, so it is time to do something about it. The day after the party, with all my flower bouquets around me, I went on this online dating website that my friend had recommended the night before.

I got very clear that I would not be doing the chasing but I would allow the men to do the chasing. I fully trusted my intuition in this dating process and I only paid for one month membership as I was super intentional that I would find the love of my life in one month. When I paid those £30, a fortune for me at the moment, I emotionally magnified that sum into the best ever investment for my life. I blessed those £30 intentionally and deep gratitude for my man to find me.

I met a guy within three days, nice, friendly but nothing more. Then, I met Richard for a coffee. It only took a couple of hours for us to feel strongly connected! So, there we are now, three weeks later. And it is getting stronger and stronger. He is half Scottish, 60 years old although he does not look his age as he does not have grey hair!

He is a gentle man. I feel very lucky! We both feel very much in love with each other. This is extremely exciting, amazing, a miracle.

Another big news: my friend Jason who has a lot of experience in book writing, editing and publishers has started reading the first draft of our book. He is super impressed and motivated. He has offered to help. We are now working on the structure via Skype.

Jason has asked me to say hi to you and tell you he is on board now. OK, mi amigo de USA & Mexico! Sempre tu amiga!

Suzanne (who is in love!)

30th March 2016

Roberto!

I am in a cafe (the sunny one and yes, there is sunshine) and yes, I am working on the book.

It dawned on me how we could have so easily missed each other. You could have found any other pen friend, but we met! I am sensing the invisible energy threads that connect people across the world even if they don't ever meet physically. Yesterday I wrote a thank you card to our coordinator for putting us in touch. I had been meaning to do this for a while.

Feeling so much gratitude.

I have been thinking about the death watch period if or when you get your execution date. It is really hard to write about this. I feel we need to already prepare you for the eventuality of that 60 – 30 days period so that your energy, frequency, wellbeing can remain as high and stable.

I am realising that if one day, we hit such a scenario, I will need support during that phase. Lifelines offers counselling. It is hard to think about this, but we need to talk about it, no?

My appreciation for you is linked to respect. I respect you. You are a strong being Robert. You have come an awful long way and are still on the way: willing, wise and funny.

It is raining today but I am going to put my waterproofs on and go for a walk before I write anymore.

I am going to start a Chinese herbal treatment to help support my adrenal glands and my energy levels. Feeling hopeful.

I am dancing a bit every day on my own here. It feels good to re-build my stamina like this. I might go Friday for a little try out again. I am going to explore a different class also.

I want to start teaching you some deeper meditation stuff so you can prepare for the death watch. I hope that we never get to that but if you do, the more able you are at connecting with your divine self, the better.

Does that feel OK, me telling you that?

Suzanne

April 2nd 2016

Suzanne,

Here is a part of the events that lead to why I am on death row.
I don't like thinking about it but here it is.

I told you I ended up living with Lily, her husband and her lover and her son Arthur. Lily shared the same bed with her two men and had threesomes. The night of the killing, her lover was at work.

One day, a van pulled up into the property and dropped off a man and a young girl who had been hitchhiking: Jake and Laura. They said they were father and daughter and needed a place to stay until Jake could find some way of getting money to get them a bus ticket to the next State where they were heading to.

Lily and Peter agreed that they could stay there for a few days to get themselves situated and figure out what they wanted to do. Now looking back, it seems strange to me for strangers to be driven to a house that was located in the middle of nowhere and ask to stay overnight. Especially after they were told that there was no electricity, no running water and the nearest town was three miles away. Maybe Jake and Laura were running away from something. This, I don't know.

Lily told them that she could take them to the health and welfare office to apply for assistance and help Jake see if he could find some odd job in town. The first night, we all talked and got to know them. Their story of being father and daughter became suspect as they didn't act like that. Jake must have been in his late forties and Laura said she was 18, only later on did I found out that she was actually 14.

The following day Lily and Peter drove Jake into town. Laura stayed back with me. As we talked I was able to confirm my suspicions. I found out they were in a romantic relationship. She explained that they told people they were father and daughter because most would judge them for their age difference. I began to flirt with her.

When Jake arrived back at the property he attempted to continue with the same story, but Laura told him I already knew the truth. Jake brought some beers with him. The three of us drank that night, laughing and carried on getting to know each other. I must admit that I was very attracted to Laura and in a way she invited the flirting when Jake wasn't around. Jake kept telling us how he had connections with the Italian mafia in the next state and that's why they were going there.

The more we drank, the more they asked questions about the others. I got angrier and angrier about the fact that I was paying the full rent and food, that they were using me.

The next day Jake said he had to go into town to check on a job. Lily and her guy agreed to take him. Laura stayed back with me and Arthur but he quickly left us alone. Laura and I took one of the dogs for a walk and got closer.

The others came back from town much later. Again Jake brought some beer back and the three of us separated ourselves and began to drink. They asked me further questions about Lily and the rest. I was getting extremely upset again. I felt that I was being robbed.

Laura expressed how much she hated being here and wanted to carry on traveling and out of nowhere she said "well, we could just kill them and take the truck". It stunned both me and Jake at how serious she was.

After that, Jake kept asking how we would do it, kill them, if we could. The rest of the night we joked and gave examples. The more we drank, the more we gave outlandish ways of how we would kill them. Eventually we broke up our little party and went to bed.

The next day Jake approached me and wanted to know if I would help if they decided to go through with the killing. I was hesitant and told him to let me think about it. As I thought about it, the rent situation fuelled me the wrong way. On some level I didn't think Jake would go through with it, so I agreed. I was also starting to make myself believe that I would be better living in the next state with Jake and Laura and his mafia connections.

Throughout the day we began planning and created many scenarios. I came up with the plan to lure Arthur into the small trailer by telling him that Laura wanted to have sex with him and that Jake wanted to watch them so he could get sexually aroused. At which both of them agreed would be perfect and that was the plan we stuck to.

The murders began a few hours later.

I don't like thinking about this.

Robert

April 14th 2016

Hi there Suzanne,

Though they are a presence in my life, I don't like to think about the murders. But I do want to tell you what happened.

First their ages: Peter was 49 years old, Lily 34 or 35 and Arthur was 15 years old. Lily was into Native American forms of spirituality and geared towards sun and Mother Earth worshiping which is more common among the American Indian. With Lily I had a few deep discussions. She was killed by a single gunshot which went through her upper lip and hit the top of her spinal cord. According to the trial it was a quick death. I shot her.

Arthur could draw anything. I was very impressed by his skill. He was a lonely and solitary kid. I spent a lot of time together with him as I pretty much was looking after him. We were at that secluded place alone most of the time. On several occasions I stayed with him for three or four days without seeing his mom or any of her two lovers.

We were like brothers and killing him was a nightmare. He died in a 45 minutes struggle. He truly suffered. Me and Jake used a bread knife to slice his throat and stabbed him in the head and used rocks to hit his head. It was a gruesome killing. It took a long time for him to die. It is one of the reasons I thought that my next life would be a bad karmic retribution.

Peter was a bit self-absorbed, he was only interested in Lily and didn't care about anyone else. I believe that Arthur was neglected and a big part was because of Peter. His mum Lily was more involved with her two lovers than with her son. Arthur was the only one who did any work around the house and fed the dogs most of the time. There weren't any real good memories with Peter. We didn't get along well. We only tolerated each other.

Peter was shot through the cheek but not killed right away. He got up and ran and was hit multiple times with a rifle barrel and then had his head smashed with a cinder block. I used the cinder block and committed most of the murder.

I killed them all.

It all started when I walked into the small trailer. Jake had Arthur in a choke hold, I was surprised and shocked. My first comment to Arthur was: "It's OK, it's a joke". But Jake said it was too late as he had already started to cut Arthur's throat. It hit me that we couldn't turn back. From that time on I was numb. I didn't feel anything.

After the killings, we got into the truck and left the property. We started to head East because Jake had convinced me that he was in the Italian mafia. It sounds stupid now but at the time I believed him.

I couldn't sleep for two days, I had nightmares. I began to get scared. I realized that I took three lives. Every time I remembered the times before the murders, I felt destroyed and when alone I would cry. I did not want to get caught. I knew that if I were caught I would die in prison. I didn't know if that particular State had the death penalty but I knew I'd never be free again, if not executed.

We drove for five days. On the 4th day Laura and I got even closer. We would kiss and fool around whenever Jake wasn't around. She was young and easy to brainwash. Jake had convinced her to run away from her family with him.

On the 5th day we were in a motel in a different state when we found out that Jake had lied to us about the mafia. He went to shower. I kissed Laura and when he came back he caught us. We got into a small fight and he left. I had sex with Laura for the first time.

The next day, we went one way and Jake left with the truck another way. For the next three days we hitchhiked and ended up in a homeless shelter. Ten days after the murders we got arrested.

Jake had been arrested before us.

I spent three weeks in a jail before I was extradited to the state where the murders had happened. Jake was also extradited back to the state of the killings. During that time in jail I got into fights and did drugs and just didn't care anymore.

On the day I was sentenced I was trying to be emotionless but after they sentenced me to death, my mom screamed and started crying. I lost it. I collapsed.

I spent the next week locked down waiting to be transferred to death row. The transfer was a six hours drive in an unmarked police car with two police officers. Getting to death row was nerve wracking. I had just turned 19. I was scared and didn't know what was going to happen. When I got to my cell I had nothing except a few papers I brought with me and hygiene articles the prison gave me. A few inmates gave me stamps and paper to write to loved ones to let them know I was here.

It is hard to share all this. I think it always will be. I know that it's important to tell you.
Robert

May 3rd 2016

Hi Suzanne,

I have written a letter to the man who raped me. I want you to burn it. After telling you about the murders, I want to free myself from my blaming him.

To Chris,

I want to send this message out into the world to release the anger, rage, hurt, feelings of betrayal and pain I have suffered since the day you raped me when I was 11 years old. For a long time, I have held onto that betrayal and horrible act.

It has affected my relationships. It has caused me to distrust all male figures growing up.

I have used drugs and alcohol to erase the memory and feelings though only temporarily.

I have caused other people pain, foolishly thinking and wanting everyone else to feel pain.

I have lashed out at my family and friends, keeping them at a distance.

I have purposely sabotaged every romantic relationship because I thought I was not worth being loved.

I have held myself at a distance from everyone who loved me.

You took advantage of a grieving little boy who for so long blamed himself for what you did to him. I blamed myself that I wasn't man enough to stop you. For most of my life I have fought with that trauma, thinking. I had to prove I was a man. I never was able to fill the void you created in me.

I have hated you, wished you the very worst. I hoped you would die suffering and alone.

The rape you committed on me devastated me, I have felt guilty for knowing that I could not have been the first or the last one.

I have been on a spiritual journey for the last eight years but only in the last one and a half year have I truly committed my life to bettering myself, to gaining knowledge, in wanting to let go of my past, learning from it and letting it go.

My anger towards you is something I have. It has held me back and so with this letter to you I release it. I hope that in your next life your karmic retribution is not too great. I hope you are able to find where your demons came from and can better yourself.

As these pages burn, I release my negative energy and open my mind and heart to the positive energy of love and knowledge. I hope that by writing this down and sharing it, I can help others come to terms with whatever traumatic event has occurred in their lives: that they all can open their hearts to the love and knowledge that the world has to offer.

With this letter I take away the power of negative energy you have brought to my life and replace it with the positive energy of love. I open my life and heart to the possibility of being loved by all those I have wronged, and I open my life to the relationships that are to come to me in this life and in all future lives.

May your next life be filled with the love you denied me and that you are able to grow as a human being.

I forgive you.
With love and positive energy I release my anger and rage.
Robert.

May 9th 2016

Hello Suzanne,

I have been thinking a lot lately about the murders and have meditated on them. I came to the realization about something I never wanted to look deeply into the manner of which each murder was committed was a symbol of my life in a way.

Lily was murdered quickly; she was female, and I have always felt closer to women.

Because of my resentment of how all men treated me. Peter and Arthur's killings were long and brutal. I think subconsciously I took out all my rage and anger for all the male figures who abused me and abandoned me. It struck me how Arthur's life was similar to mine. I didn't know his past too well but his present was similar to mine. He was abandoned by the adults around him.

I saw my younger self in Arthur and how weak I was for not stopping the rape and all other physical abuses I endured. Although it is Arthur who died in my rage, I didn't see him — I was seeing myself. I killed my weak child.

After his brutal and long death, my rage grew even bigger and the other two murders happened.
I think this explains the ways in which they were killed.
I am still trying to work this out.

I am still trying to understand.
Robert

Reflecting on Our Friendship

Integrating the Murders

When I first read about Robert's murders through the prison's website and his legal confession, I was disturbed. But to read what Robert had done in his own words hit me the hardest. I felt a rage and hatred unequalled in my life. It was especially the gruesome killing of a teenage boy that repulsed me the most.

Although my rage and hatred have since left me, I still have the same reaction every time I re-read about the killings. I get a chill down my spine; I feel a deep sense of unease. It leaves me drained for a while. But my biggest reaction to those murders is absolute disbelief — disbelief that a fourteen-year-old girl could trigger two men into killing three innocent people. This is beyond my understanding.

Here are my words at the time to Robert; I am not proud of them:

"I am struggling with forgiving you. Not just the killings but mainly for Arthur's killing and the way you killed him. A butchering. The fact that he was a child. The fact that you knew him. The fact that you liked him like a brother.

I feel hatred. I hate you for that act. I hate that act. I almost hate myself for being a part of your story, that story.

I cannot forgive you. I know I will, I know I want to. I almost feel you deserve death row. I almost feel you deserve execution which goes against all my values and beliefs!

I understand that as I-your friend, cannot forgive you-my friend, then who in society can? I understand why death row exists, because it is so hard to forgive or even simply accept.

How could you do that?

It makes me feel sad. I want to cry. I want to weep, for you and for that child, for the one who killed and for the ones who got killed.

I also want to thank you for this opportunity where I have to dig deeper inside my humanity, go deeper into forgiveness, compassion, unconditional love, acceptance.

I know I will be able to enter forgiveness and release my hatred. At some point, I will. But right now, I can't.

I am sorry, please forgive me, thank you, I love you."

Several days later, I was able to be more constructive in my writing:

"I have been reflecting, integrating, praying the Hawaiian way. My struggle to forgive you is still here. It is a question of morality, moral issues. It is a question of inhumanity. This is crucial. It is fascinating as we are co-authoring a book about the potentiality of being human, and your act of killing Arthur is inhuman. This is where I am stuck right now. This is not easy. You killed two adults, but I am haunted by the slaughter of Arthur. I am repulsed beyond comprehension.

Of course, you don't deserve death row, you don't deserve execution, you don't deserve life imprisonment especially as you have changed. I know soon I hope, one day, I will forgive you.

Thank you, Robert, for forcing me to evolve, to grow, to be more human myself. In fact, who am I am to judge?

You are my spiritual teacher right now. You are forcing me to understand more profound layers of compassion and acceptance."

At the time, I was surprised that Robert got angry and confused at my reaction. I expected him to be more understanding. I think being a murderer and living with other murderers has, maybe, desensitised him to the fact that killing people is not the norm.

Looking back now, I regret my reactions and at the same time I don't. It helped me voice my truth and it was our brutal honesty that allowed us both to process and integrate into our friendship, this challenging fact about his past. We both said what had to be said and no grey areas remained unspoken. I came to understand that it was not my place to forgive him but the only person who could forgive Robert was himself. We painfully were able to transform our friendship.

I admit, it is not easy to embrace that my friend had been a slaughtering killer! I still feel for the family and friends of the victims. In my idealism, there is a part of me that would like to be their friend, through letter writing, even if it was just to say "I am sorry". But it is not the case. I just hope that throughout the years they received the support they needed and wanted.

Robert's life certainly reveals how he himself was a victim of neglect, violence, abuse, and rape since he was a young boy. His years in youth rehabilitation centres certainly did nothing to help him heal his wounds so he could create a different life for himself. His crimes were his cries for help. No one properly heard him until it was too late.

The naked truth that frames Robert and my involvement with him, will always be that three people lost their lives because of him. This can never be changed, erased, ignored or overlooked. It is always there, so is his status of death row inmate waiting for his execution. These two facts remain as something to be accepted, embraced and integrated. There is no going around those two essentials.

I still find it difficult to accept Robert's wholeness—to see the wonderful person he is and include at the same time, the extreme concept that he brutally killed three people. It is one of those contradictions of life which pushes me into grace, the grace of transcending acceptance. Those two contradictions exist simultaneously. It is the only way for me to befriend Robert in his totality, his full humanity, to see him completely.

My biggest on-going life lesson is we are all composed of light and shadow, the beautiful yin and yang incarnated in each one of us.

Facts of the past cannot be changed, death takes our loved ones away, we will all die one day, one way or another, some peaceful, some brutal. What matters is how we live each moment, and this is where Robert shines his own light. Every time I read his latest letter, I am touched by his spirit and wisdom. I am forever reminded that he is a human being, worthy of love.

I was mad at Suzanne for what she wrote. I replied back:
"I want to be honest about my reaction to reading what you wrote. I am mad, confused and hurt. Confused because I thought you knew what happened, but I am assuming that the fact that it was me, my words saying struck you the most. Mad and hurt because of you are saying you don't know if you could forgive me for what I did to Arthur and that you feel that I deserve death row and that if you, my friend, cannot forgive me, what about society at large. This surprised me because they are strong emotions. Of course, those were your reactions before you could reflect. I hate that you even thought what you thought.

The reality Suzanne is I struggle everyday knowing that I was part of those murders. I know I am not that person anymore. I was a different person back then. I was taking drugs and drinking. I was full of hatred. I didn't care who got hurt or how badly. I was suffering so I wanted the world to suffer. This was the attitude I had.

Now, I have to live with the fact that I am responsible for the deaths of three people, two of whom were brutally done, one being a child. I realize the killings were horrible, disgusting, and deplorable. I live with this nightmare every day, and yes, it is a question of morality and inhumanity but back then I didn't care.

Because I walk a spiritual path I must face those deaths. I can't prepare for whatever comes next without making peace with them. I cannot change that past. And in the end, I know there will be karmic retribution. I fully accept that, no matter what it will be".

I don't like to look back on the murders, the person I was then. Even at the time, I would never have imagined ever killing anyone. For a long time, I lived with the "What if's". What if Jake and Laura had never arrived at the property, what would my life be like?

I think the way I was living at the time would have eventually led to incarceration or death. I know this because at that time I didn't care about anything except the anger, rage and hatred that were festering inside me. There was a small window in which there was some hope of change but it came too late.

My hope was that about a week before Laura and Jake arrived I had called an ex-girlfriend and discussed the possibility of me moving up with her. I was working for a few weeks for a temporary work agency to earn enough money for me to go and live with her. She had said yes to us starting over again, but I had to wait for my pay cheque to be sent to me. That cheque was due to arrive a little over a week after Laura and Jake landed in my life and the murders occurred.

Do I think the murders would have happened if Laura had never suggested that we kill them and take the truck? A hard question to answer but as I meditated on it, I came to the conclusion that a lot of things went wrong the night she suggested it. If we hadn't been drinking the idea would have never formed in her head or at least that is what I believe. The truth is I don't think it would have happened.

Suzanne has asked me if I blame Laura and Jake for what happened. For a long time, I did, I wanted to believe that if they hadn't arrived it would never have happened and truthfully it probably wouldn't have. It took me a long time to face the reality that there is enough blame to go around. In order for me to grow and help others I must take responsibility for my actions, my part in the murders and in the end the person I must blame is myself, I could have said NO!!!

I have been able to evolve my feeling about why I am on death row. I wish I could open a dialogue with the families of the three people I am responsible for taking the lives of. I know there will never be any words I could say to take away their pain or fill the void of their loss, but I think it would help them to know why their loved ones were taken from them. I will never make excuses for what happened because there is never going to be one that is sufficient enough to justify the actions of me taking their lives

Who We Have Become

That secret desire I held over five years ago that I would create the cause by my commitment to be Robert's friend for life, to find my beloved certainly reaped great fruit. I have been with the love of my life, Richard, for four years now! It makes me smile when I look back on how I had announced that major event to Robert. Our love birthed itself within a couple of hours. I literally saw his aura turn green and pink as we were sharing lunch on our first date and the thought "this man has just fallen in love with me" flashed my mind. Richard also remembers the exact moment when he perceived that I had fallen in love with him, during that same lunch.

After two and a half years of religiously seeing each other every single weekend and often during the week and holidays, we finally moved in together. This move was a big shift and my life has truly blossomed in spectacular and unplanned areas that are making me profoundly happy and fulfilled.

We live in a magical little house, along a canal that crosses London. From our windows, we view the canal boats passing by, often playing funky jazz or loud party music, we hear the lively sounds of the seagulls, geese, coot hens, ducks, and can catch sights of herons and cormorants. I am very happy here.

After meeting Richard and being so deeply, madly, powerfully, happily in love, my priorities drastically changed. My focus turned to him and our love. Slowly but surely, I started to meditate less. My mystical and spiritual experiences came from our making love. We are fortunate to resonate harmoniously on many levels and one being sexually. This became my primary form of spiritual awareness, ecstatically, delightfully shared with the man I love. My soul has been touched within my feminine body by his masculine body. Often, we are doing nothing more than allowing something bigger and more powerful than us, to take over. Our bliss takes me to places I didn't even know existed.

This new chapter of sexual spirituality blew my mind, body and soul. I observed my old meditations disappear and accepted the natural ebbs and flows of ways of exploring conscious awareness. I observed Robert diligently carrying on with his meditations, his regular fasting, his wows of improvement. Sometimes I felt ashamed of not meditating anymore, I almost felt I was betraying our shared spirituality. I really admire this in Robert, his relentless commitment to his evolution.

Richard is dyslexic and dyspraxic. This was the biggest challenge in the early days of our relationship. I did not understand what would happen to him daily which sets him apart from "normal" human reactions and actions. I love a man who is neurologically different! This is his greatest gift; this is the part of him I love the most and it is also the part which exacerbates me the most. I admire him for having created ways to cope and blossom. I am still learning to fully embrace his unusual ways.

Funnily enough, Richard finds me the most atypical person he has ever known; with my daily ups and downs of energy, one day I can walk, the next day I am too weak to walk, my numerous moods and emotions, my psychic abilities. We are a good pair, two oddities, a good match!

After leaving my assistant manager job at the charity shop four years ago, I wanted to work as a palliative carer in a hospice. I looked up the hospice near me and surprisingly they were looking for healthcare assistants. I did not have any qualifications, but I applied knowing I had knowledge and experiences around dying and death. During the interview, it was clear that they were looking for someone who could handle such an environment and death as it were! I got the job.

I worked there for two years and witnessed first-hand the dying process of hundreds of people. I have taken care of dead bodies, seen beauty and ugly beyond what we are commonly used to. I have been exposed to damaged bodies: cancers that deform, brain tumours that steal the personality, neuro motor conditions that rob all capacities. One man had no more testicles, no penis, no anus and no belly button. They all had been surgically removed in order to give him a few weeks of extra life. Instead, he had oozing scars and tubes. I would hold his hand and listen to his seriously damaged psyche. He died a tormented soul in a mutilated body.

One needs nerves of steel and a heart of diamond to accompany someone on their dying journey. Once, a young man in his thirties came back from receiving radiotherapy and his pain was so extreme that our state-of-the-art pain control systems could not help him. I stayed sitting next to him and holding him whilst he yelled in agony. After that, every time he saw me, he would say in French "je t'adore", I adore you. This kind of love and bond is priceless. My special friend died soon after.

I have witnessed grace. I have seen and felt it, especially in people who die young in their twenties and thirties. There is an acceptance, a transcendence that manifests as grace. I feel tearful thinking about them.

There are so many stories I could share that have touched the core of my soul. A young woman for instance, in her mid-twenties, an opera singer. Her mum and boyfriend practically lived with her in her room. I took care of her. She looked like a frail bird, stunning in its fragility. I wanted to speak to her beyond her immediate care.

Often, I would just pop in to say hello. I felt I knew her. We were both Celtic.

My frail bird deteriorated quickly. The night she died, I was on a late shift and looked after her. Her room was overfilled with her friends and family, her mum and boyfriend right by her side. She was in agony. She laid, a twisted skeleton of a foetal bird. We knew she was within hours of death. I would go in, pass the crowd, caress her softly, speak to her gently almost telepathically.

I felt crushingly impotent, powerless. It was unbearable. I wanted to give her my best—my loving presence. That night, there was an almighty summer's thunderstorm, torrential rain, violent thunder, her farewell symphony. She had sung operas after all. She died accompanied by a gigantic natural orchestra. Our connection was only a mere blink of time but I was there for my Celtic sister's death. It crushed me.

One lady transformed her room into an art gallery. She stayed with us for nearly four months after arriving from hospital where she had been within moments of death but instead of dying she had miraculously reverted back to life. She painted relentlessly. She glued glitter onto canvases, spread colours. Her husband exuded an otherworldly wisdom, an aura of spiritual beauty. His understanding of death was profound. I admired how he handled the situation. We hoped that she would live and be cured, but the signs of decline appeared eventually.

One morning upon entering her room, I found her husband sitting by her side, holding her hand. He simply said "she just died". I saw her shining light. What a moment. I held him, touched her hand and remained stunned by the incredible ethereal beauty and light that exuded from her entire being. We stayed there, out of time and space. Her husband spoke words of wisdom and declared his love for her. I became acutely aware that I was living an extraordinarily privileged moment, a unique transcending experience.

There were so many of those moments. All kinds of patients, the humorous ones, the tricky ones, the aggressive ones, the unconscious ones — the full spectrum of human conditions and personalities. Some die alone, many in fact. No family, no friends, estranged. Accompanying people in their final departure, being there as a loving and healing presence was the most precious gift I could give and the most rewarding of my work. I felt magic and beauty when I would patiently create the right situation to generate a blissful, precious laughter in a dying person. Yes, it is possible, and some rekindle their spark even if it is just for a few seconds.

However, the most difficult aspect followed soon after: to wash and bag their dead bodies. I will always remember this young man in his early thirties who had just died. He was plain gorgeous. Together with a male nurse we washed and bagged his body. We took our time, just the three of us, in that dim room, curtains closed. We looked at his beautiful young face, we spoke to him, we stayed in reverent silence, we honoured his life and his passing. We washed him in grace, in presence. We loved him in an unexplainable manner, a love that is only felt in that unique soulful space with a still warm, dead person.

Then came the most traumatic part: bagging the body and putting it into the fridge, as I would call our mortuary. We did this brutal act by taking our time, not zipping the bag in one go, still touching "him", touching his heart area one final time, saying final words, then zipping the last centimetres. We stayed looking at his bagged body. It was a cruel sight.

Sliding a bagged body into its fridge slot is no easy task. You need to push hard! And how do you push when you have known this person, loved them in your own way whilst they were dying? I would pray and express words out loud. But I never, never got it right. Shoving a dead body into those fridges systematically traumatised me. Then, I would go back to the ward as if it all was normal. But often, I had to take discretionary time off, go for a walk in the hospice's garden or sit in the prayer room.

Once a person is deemed dead, their body becomes an object. At best it will be treated as a sacred object to be honoured; at worst, it will be dealt with mechanically, quickly and without emotions. Would it not be so much easier if when we die, the body dissipates in a puff of subtle smoke? Poof, gone. There would be no fridge, no body bags. But this is not the case. Nope, corpses remain, and we live in a culture where we are uncomfortable around such blatant proof of our mortality.

One time, I was stunned at how this male head nurse carefully wrapped a body in a bed sheet. I had never seen this done before. It was a revelation — something I had been craving for: a way to properly, decently, reverently wrap and hold a human corpse. He told me this is how he had been taught in Scotland. I could have cried in joy. It made the bagging less inhumane and harsh. A shroud ritual!

I hope to have made some impact on the clinical team as I eventually raised with the head of our wards that to disrupt a person who is in the window, as the clinical team would call the few hours or days of active dying, to systematically wash them, change their clothing or just refresh them was not just ludicrous but scandalous. I have observed the worst violent reactions of shock and trauma in people being disrupted in their dying process. It is traumatic to witness such violation. Slowly but surely, the nurses started to also question the need for this. I voiced my opposition to such practices as I felt we were robbing the patient of their unique dying journey. This, in my view, is terrible, a crime against humanity.

I would have lots to say about what I think of the modern hyper medicated approach to dying in the Western world but suffice to say that I truly believe that if each citizen was exposed to how natural and special dying is and should be, that society would drastically change for the better.

However, death remains a taboo. The death penalty remains legal in many countries. Economically justified wars are still deemed acceptable. Most people are afraid of their own death. What is wrong with the modern human psyche?

Meanwhile, Robert, from his death row, remained a steadfast companion. I would share my stories with him, and he would send me back his blessings and wise views. He would often tell me that he was holding me in his energy and love from afar. It helped to have such a friend.

My work at the hospice began to have its toll. It takes time to integrate such magnitude of intense moments. The gifts I received I can only wish for everyone else, but they came with a price and I paid it. After nearly two years, I functioned like a zombie, my perimenopause symptoms got worse including hormonal insomnia. I felt exhausted beyond belief. I would be at work with only four hours max of broken sleep. I would get home and just go to bed. I felt ninety years old, not fifty three! To work in the palliative field, one has to be wholly fit, if not, it is a serious peril to one's well-being. My work was, by then damaging me physically and emotionally. I could not carry on. I handed in my notice; my shifts were cancelled.

I stopped work and started to bleed for four months. After weeks and months, one cannot call it a period anymore. It was plain awful and worrying. I became depressed. My mood grew pretty dark. I entered a long dark night of the soul.

Giving up work and putting my health first was the best decision ever. It led Richard and I to go deeper in our love as from that point for nearly a year and a half I wasn't capable of doing any of my spiritual work either. I had to learn to accept his abundance as mine. I had to open up to not view myself as dependent on him financially but embrace that we dance to the give and receive tempo of life together. That dance beats many rhythms and melodies.

Perimenopause made me emotionally hyper unstable: one minute rageful, the next tearful or passively lethargic. When I coined the term "madness" it really helped. It freed me to honestly tell my friends that I was falling into madness. The torture of not sleeping, night after night took its toll. I wanted to die so I could sleep. I became obsessed with how to kill myself so that I could finally sleep! To cope and stay afloat, I tried sleeping tablets, but they made me sick. I tried many herbal tablets, liquids, teas, infusions, some worked a little, for a little while.

I managed to organise a few Menopause Café meetings through the Menopause Café movement which proved deeply enlightening. I thought I was going through a tough time but some of the other women had stories to make you shudder. I know that some women sail through their cycle ending but I did not, and many don't.

Looking back, I am so grateful that I allowed myself to endure my long dark night of the soul. Unconscious patterns unravelled and came to the surface to be heard, seen, held and healed. It was a dangerous time as I did not know if I would have the strength to remain sufficiently aware without doing something drastically self-destructive.

Some nights, I would perceive the shadow of the Akashic field of women. I felt the layers still held in the great Unconscious Mind of women pretending to be something they are not, hiding their true selves. Those many months of darkness have transformed who I am. They have birthed and aligned my soul with my spirit. I am free.

In the middle of such daily ordeal, of waking up late, feeling utterly shit and worse than when I went to bed the previous evening, feeling blank and brain fried, I started to draw first thing in the morning as a means to find my sanity and to do something healing, soothing.

Drawing was keeping me afloat. It kept me so buoyant that I started noticing that when I was in that creative space, I became alive. I lost track of time, of who I am, of what was happening. I became lost in colours, in lines, on paper and I fell seriously in love with that space of beingness.

A force took over which allowed my natural childlike curiosity to see beauty and wonder in what could be the banal for others. Using my hands and trusting this spirited joy to take over shifted me into my happiest state of being. My essence became revealed, who I am at my core: an artist. I feel a bit shy saying this, since it can sound such a grand, snobbish word "an artist". It is amazing how in my first letter to Robert, I had introduced myself as "a bit of an artist".

Throughout my life, I have enjoyed painting and drawing. But this time, it felt stronger. I felt flooded with a growing sense that this creative space is me. This came as a revelation. Even writing this book became a creative process, I became an artist using words rather than colours. It helped me keep our book alive as I wanted to give it up at the height of my unwellness. Robert had categorically refused!

As my artist path unfolded and blossomed, I feared that I was leaving my spiritual one. For a long while, it bothered me as I didn't have an answer to how those two could co-exist. Then one evening, I was drawing among people in the exhibition we created with two other friends (a poetess and a photographer), and I felt one hundred percent in my power, trusting every line, every movement coming out of my hand onto the paper, unfazed by who was looking at me or not — I was completely in a spiritual flow. Eureka! My path as an artist is still my spiritual path.

My artist seed sprouted so beautifully and effortlessly that I am now applying to do an arts foundation course. When I dared tell Richard that I was thinking of studying art and becoming more involved in my creativity, his wonderful response was "This is so you. It makes total sense."

Friends for Life

Who would have thought that throughout the first five years of our friendship so many things would have changed? It has been a bumpy road, a lot more good times than bad ones. I have had many obstacles on the way, but it certainly has been a wonderful journey.

Let me start with my daughter. In September of 2016 I received a letter from my now ex-wife asking me for a divorce. I agreed and as a divorce present, she went on Facebook and searched through hundreds of profiles to see if she could match certain facts together that would fit my daughter's. She eventually found a young woman that looked almost like me. It turned out to be my daughter!

I gave my mom her information and within a week they were in contact. If it had been just them communicating, I would have been happy, because I would have known that my little girl had the opportunity to be part of my side of the family. However, I got much more than that. I was able to connect with her too and within a few months Jen decided to move to the state my family lives in.

I called home to check in with my mom. When the phone was picked up, I was concerned as it wasn't the usual voice that I heard, so I thought maybe she had a cold, or her allergies were acting up. The voice asked "Do you know who this is?" I responded that yeah it was mom and the voice said "No, this is your daughter!" I can freely admit that my eyes welled up and I had to quickly find something to sit on as my legs became weak. I felt a huge elation at knowing I was speaking to my daughter, that for the first time in our lives I was hearing her voice and she was hearing mine. This was something that I had only dreamed of for a long time. I, of course, spent the whole call talking to her and immediately called back after the first 15 minutes were done. It was an odd sensation to talk to her but I was filled with so much joy.

Later when I talked to my mom she explained how it was all set up. Apparently my daughter moved in with my mom within the first month of them being in contact but they kept it a secret from me. They agreed they would surprise me.

Getting to know Jen has been the most amazing thing but at times a bit heart breaking. For example, when cousins and aunts found out that she was moving close to them they all flocked to my mom's place to meet her and with us being the typical Mexican family they immediately hugged and kissed her cheeks. In a later conversation with Jen I found out that this initial meeting had scared her because she wasn't used to such affection.

It saddened me to know that she was unfamiliar with this kind of love. I must also admit that I was surprised my family reacted like they did as I had assumed some would treat her not as warmly because of their feelings towards me. But amazingly they embraced her.

My relationship with her has grown and soon we will be welcoming two new members to the family. She is currently engaged and pregnant. At 44 years old I will be a grandfather to a little girl who will have as her middle name my mom's name.

The changes in my life have impacted me greatly but I continue to hold on to my growing spiritual beliefs. A new aspect I have learned is that if I surround myself with positive people, my life begins to improve and good things begin to happen.

One important lesson I have learned is that I can always improve myself and no matter how prepared I think I am there will always be something new I can learn to better myself. The more knowledge and wisdom I gain in this life, the more it will guide me in the next.

One of the biggest changes that happened to my section of death row is that we were moved from a maximum security unit to a closed custody unit that has allowed us more freedom and privileges. Only some of us were selected to move based on our past behaviour.

As you know from my letters, I lived until then in a lockdown unit. We were locked down 24/7 and could only leave our cells after we were stripped searched with our hands cuffed behind us until we were in a secure room, then the door was shut and closed behind us. Then the cuffs were taken off. Even to walk the 15 to 20 feet to the shower required us to be handcuffed.

In 2015, two prisoners began the process of filing a lawsuit on our behalf over the inhumane way we were being treated and to keep us locked down in solitary confinement with no human contact other than the little we had with the guards when they put handcuffs on us. The argument for the lawsuit being that it was unconstitutional, cruel and that every other prisoner that is on lockdown status should be given the opportunity to work their way through classes and programs to lower their prison score and thus making them eligible to be transferred to a lower custody level unit.

Finally in early 2017 the prison decided that it was cheaper to move the prisoners that qualified to a lower prison unit. Finally after many months of nerve testing wait, we were moved to a lower custody level and here we are.

The move was challenging as we had been left for so long in some grey area to whether the move would really happen or not. It took me a long time to adapt to being able to move around and being in places with others. I felt overwhelmed. I stayed in my cell and gradually started to make use of the new layout.

For the first weeks I was confused as to what to do with my hands. I spent close to 19 years in the maximum security unit and was accustomed to not moving out of my cell without my hands being cuffed behind me.

I chose to be in a single person cell when I could have chosen to share one with another person. I thought about it a lot and came to the conclusion that after about twenty years alone in isolation, I could not cope with sharing a cell. We are able to work within the perimeter of the unit. I am now a laundry porter. There is a room attached to the run I am on and it has a washer and dryer. I collect laundry in the morning and do it for other prisoners. I am paid 30¢ an hour, I work eight hours a day and every two weeks I receive $24 in my banking account. Because of my job I have more freedom than most.

Some more perks and privileges we get now. In the other unit our food was brought to our cells, in this unit we all go to a dining hall to pick up our food, we do this twice a day. We are also given three hours of table time, this basically means that all the doors are opened and we are able to socialize with other prisoners. Because we are the calmest prison population the guards tend to give us extra time. I adapted to this new freedom over time as there was too much noise, too much movement, too many people. But now I like it.

In the end the move has been positive and for the most part there aren't any fights. The majority of the people who came over to this unit have been locked down for 10 years or more and absolutely don't want to sacrifice the privileges and perks that we have now. A lot of guards want to work in our building because they know not a lot of drama goes on here.

With all of that, I must also tell you that death row will be moving again to a high medium unit. The governor of our state has made it his mission to empty out this unit and three other ones. Apparently, it cost too much money to continue doing repairs and so sometime between now and the middle of next year, death row will once again be moved. If they move us to the medium security unit, we will be afforded even more privileges. I will have to find a new job because I don't think they'll allow me to take the washer and dryer with me. :-)

Unfortunately, I have had three great losses. I lost my two great matriarchs, my grandma and her sister. They were the strength in the family and they kept us all together. I didn't know my grandma's sister but I am aware that she was greatly loved and respected.

There were a lot of turbulent years with my grandma when I was growing up. But I am grateful that we were able to heal our past and I was able to forgive her and receive her forgiveness. In the end she died of heart failure, but my mom said that she believed that grandma just missed her sister and wanted to be reunited in the next journey of life.

The third tragic loss is my mom. It has been a difficult loss as she was my rock. She was the person I would call when I was angry or feeling down. Hearing her voice reminded me of why I am on the path of evolution I am on.

I was able to see her one last time through a compassion video visit. It was hard seeing her as she was barely lucid. The family had held off her pain medication so she could have some consciousness whilst being with me. Had I known I wouldn't have set up the video visit. But I am now thankful as I believe that she didn't want to let go until she was able to be with all her children. Though she wasn't lucid nor coherent I know she could hear me because when I talked to her she perked up and her eyes opened. I told her I loved her, that I was grateful to have her as a mom and I would be fine so she could let go and be reunited with her own mother. I called the next day in the evening and was told she had passed away.

Though her loss has hit me hard, I am glad to know that in the last few years we have been able to patch up our relationship. We talked about the past and were able to make peace with both of our faults—me not being the best son and her not being a perfect mother. In all honesty though there is no such thing as a perfect son or mother. I was able to accept that she did the best that she could and I will never fault her for any mistakes. I know I wasn't the easiest child growing up and

I put her through so much. I am glad that I was able to mend things with her and that she was able to know her granddaughter.

I miss her. I had a hard time adjusting to her not being here and on days that I am feeling down or depressed I still find myself wanting to ask for the phone so I can call her to hear her voice.

It took me a long time to realize that my mom did the best she could.

Friends for Life

As I sit here in my cell writing this, it has been a little over five years since I first met Suzanne. I hope that the future will continue to bring us together and strengthen our bond.

Before she came into my life, I was so naively sure I had my life set. But destiny had other plans, and in enters Suzanne, a woman who knows nothing about the criminal side of life but with a heart I consider as gold. She begins our friendship and is willing to take the chance to write to someone who has lived his life hating everyone including himself. But I think fates did see that I had changed and had reached as far as I could spiritually with the tools I had so they sent me Suzanne. My life has been changed forever since.

As we began to write this book, we had so many goals and though they remain the same, for me with the way the world is going especially here in America we need a lot more people like Suzanne who are able to look past the negatives of a person and see their redeeming qualities.

Throughout last year there was a problem with the mail getting to and from each other. Often, I would be waiting for a letter and not receive one for a long time. I found out that Suzanne had written but only a few letters arrived.

Thankfully we have e-letters now which makes communication much easier. But I think what Suzanne said to me once is true, writing through technology does take some of the personal touch out of it. She recently made me aware that my communication has changed and that I seem more impersonal, an aspect on which I will improve on.

I am still in awe with who Suzanne is. I am particularly impressed with the changes I have seen in her new life and in her spiritual growth. I see that she continues to work on improving herself.

For five years now, Robert and I have been writing faithfully to each other and it amuses me to observe that even though we have never met nor spoken, our friendship has gone through the same ups and downs, cycles and turns like any other one. At times, it has been reassuring to accept that level of normality in what remains an unusual connection.

Letter writing is no easy commitment. It is time consuming, it hurts your fingers and it is frustrating as the handwriting is so much slower than typing. Then you need to make the time to walk to the post office or remember to post the actual letter. The number of times, I had a letter all sealed but the actual posting would take me several days. I would either forget the letter at home or was not close to a post office. I went through phases, especially when I was not working and struggled financially, I felt resentful about the cost of stamps for my USA letters, and especially for the Lifelines quarterly magazine!

However, letter writing is such a unique gift that no email, text or WhatsApp can ever come close to. There is a quality of connection and revealing that is intrinsically linked to the slow pace, the physical demands of pen and paper. Nothing can equal this. Nothing can beat the inner world that opens during the time taken to be present in the art of handwriting a letter. Nothing can beat the quality of opening a newly received letter, witnessing the known formation of the words like a drawing, touching the paper like you are touching the life of someone who resides on the other side of the world and has touched that same piece of paper. This is a unique, priceless, rewarding commitment.

I never imagined that our communication could be interfered and tampered by external forces. But last year it did. I only received three letters. Robert only got some of my letters. At one point, Robert suspected another inmate to be receiving them. The second time he reviewed our manuscript, it disappeared when he posted it back to me. The thirty plus dollars it cost to post it was a fortune for him. I even considered the end of our friendship due to the lack of communication possibilities. It felt odd to be left in limbo, not knowing how Robert was, nor what the hell was going on.

Even our Lifelines coordinator sent emails mentioning that numerous inmates and their pen friends were complaining that mail was not arriving. But she explained that Lifelines is in no position to put pressure on the prison or ask for clarification. This made me realise that my letters entering the bunker of death row is always a miracle.

Recently, Robert told me that the prison has finally issued them with tablets, and he is able to send and receive e-letters via a prison communication system. This is for sure a solution, although our e-letters are still potentially read by the prison. This e-option triggered in me a layer of resistance because yes, I am full of those layers of small fears. Certain disruptions to my habits are not easy for me. I felt resistance to what for many would just be insignificant or plain cool.

When I discuss my connection to Robert with friends or acquaintances, I find myself, time and again, in odd scenarios. Most people are fascinated by our friendship and are enthusiastic about the writing of our book and want to read it. Some have cried upon hearing of Robert's life, moved by his ordeals, inspired by his spirit.

Many admire me as if I am super courageous. But I do not feel super anything. I am simply myself. I seem to have the capacity to go where most of us don't tread. It is a personality trait of mine which can be both a blessing and a curse.

Only one friend has written to Robert, Jason who keeps an eagle eye on how our book unfolds. My mum sent Robert a postcard as she wanted to share a little comment around his bird baths as she has the same practise. For sure, I am acutely aware how it is not everyone's cup of tea to have a friend who is a death row inmate.

I have also faced virulently angry reactions for being involved with a convicted murderer. I can understand that. Others can display a slight judgmental, superior attitude to why on earth have I not been to the USA to meet him or spoken to him on the phone. I have felt judgmental and cynical about such reactions. I feel criticised so in my head I criticise back, my inner voice goes: "Well, do you write to an inmate? Oh no! Absolutely not!" I have come to view this as quite funny by now. Maybe it is simply a form of reassurance for themselves: I could be doing better! And they are right too!

Having Robert in my life is having an atypical friend for sure. He is the only person I have a connection with whilst having never seen him nor spoken to him. He is a friend I might never hug. He is probably going to be executed one day. This is no common friendship, yet it is a friendship which nourishes me in many ways.

For various reasons, I have never sent money to Robert. The process to send money is complicated. Nothing is simple when it comes to having something enter the bunker named death row. I trust his self-sufficiency and resourcefulness. But if one day, he finds himself broke I would surely help like I would any other friend.

I have never made peace with Robert's possible execution. At some point, I had to become clear to what my plan of action would be in such an eventuality. After gaining clarity that I would not go to the States for that gruesome event, I decided to stay at home to serve his soul to the best of my abilities by staying grounded. I would also seek counselling before and after with Lifelines. I would certainly rally my friends to hold me in their awareness and Robert in his transition. I have discussed all this with Robert and needless to say it was no easy conversation. I am still in disbelief that a country like the USA still has the death penalty in place and that Robert could be legally murdered!

Recently, I attended my second Lifelines local meeting which is run several times a year. It is an informal gathering of pen friends who share their stories, concerns, thoughts. It helps to meet other writers, it helps to feel not so lonely in the practise of having a death row inmate as a friend.

It made me aware of how open-minded, sane and in tune Robert is. I discovered that not all writers share such a bond with their penfriend. Hearing others, I realised what an open connection we share.

There were ladies with decades of experience writing to inmates, visiting them and going through the process of their executions. Tears guaranteed! One lady shared that she went to the US for her friend's execution. She met his entire family and was welcomed like a friend of the family as simple as that. Tears again! This made me reflect that Robert does not live family-less. He has a family, a daughter, his brothers, aunts, cousins. One day, I might meet them, who knows.

Robert had said to me that when he dies all my letters would go to his daughter. Wow, that made me feel uneasy! I seriously meditated on this and eventually accepted that my letters are his and he is free to decide what to do with them. Now, I am moved that he values our friendship and our communication so much that he would want to gift them to the most important person in his life. With Robert, I am always learning to open my heart a bit more.

At that Lifelines meeting, another lady disclosed that she had been writing to her friend for five years, that she is fifty-five years old and that she saw as a teenager a documentary about death row that shook her so much that she knew all her life that she would write to an inmate. I listened in disbelief to her as this is exactly like my own story.

She knew the name of that documentary my mum had taken me to watch a long time ago. This documentary "Fourteen days in May" was also seen by Jan Arriens who was also so moved by it that he founded Lifelines. It is amazing how one documentary, one voice can impact the world.

I felt a full circle had been completed.

This is the power of speaking our truth and reaching out.

As Robert said, in his first letter, it is never too late.

Epilogue

In August 2020, I got the news from our Lifelines coordinator, that the state where Robert is incarcerated has established access to a supplier for the third drug for the three-drug protocol for execution. The Governor simply needs to approve.

Upon reading her email, I felt a pain in my solar plexus.

Gratitude

Friends and important people in our lives come in many shapes and forms. Some stay only for a short while whilst others stay almost forever. I want to bear witness, share my appreciation and spread my deepest thank you to the following:

Consciousness itself is the first to receive my full wave of gratitude. Consciousness, an enigma, a force, the grand orchestrator of love, life, energy, spirit. Some call it God, others Source, I do too, but for today, I want to feel it as LIFE. Thank you. Life is my best friend.

The many volunteers who make LifeLines an unassuming yet powerful organisation. Thank you.

My daughter for being a strong girl, strong young woman now, for looking after me when I was so unwell for all those years, for using your passion as a force to seek and to fulfil your values. For pushing me to be the best person I can be. Thank you. You rock!

My family across England, France, Germany, Haiti. Thank you. We get along pretty well. We are one. We are lucky.

The love of my life. You pushed me, yes, annoyingly to "get it done" as you kept repeating and you were right. Thank you for your incredible grounded force of love, belief and sense of humour. That you came into my life and that we journey together remains an unfolding joy and fascinating daily miracle to be cherished each single day. Thank you. I love you man.

Jason, for giving generously of your time, efforts, beliefs into me, this book and Robert. Your presence is always powerful, simple beingness. Thank you for your vision of creating a play out of the book. Yes, I see it too on stage! Thank you for our many ten o'clock, six days a week, morning editing sessions. I have grown as a person and as a writer from them. I appreciate your honest kick up my butt! You are a precious being on this planet.

My "Steiner mums" Tara, Carole, Leila, Tricia, Jasmin, Emilie you shine brightly your unique light on the landscape of my life. You have kept me afloat when at my lowest and you celebrate my highs. So, rock on.

Guillaume and Evan for consistently believing in me.

My sparkly, super-duper upbeat girlfriends: Kate (mwoah!), Nina, Sophie (thank you for taking the photos of the illustrations, Robert's letters and cards for the book), Louise and those who will appear in the future. I thank you in advance.

Pandora for saying "well done" out of the blue with the utmost effort on your deathbed. This became my motto. What a gift! Thank you beautiful you.

My other friends who are no longer in this plane, may my love reach you on the other side of the veil: Carl, Jean-Pierre, Maurice, Mandy. A moment of silence.

Friends who come and go, you are more important than you realise. You know who you are.

Deborah Tash, thank you for appearing like a god sent coach at the perfect moment. Your generosity shines.

All the spiritual teachers, the known ones, the famous ones and the anonymous ones (you reader), walking upon our Earth with the mission to awaken as many people as they can, into the awareness of our full potential aligned to love, compassion, kindness. Vicky Clark from Ireland, thank you for teaching me how to see my own power and incarnate it with self-respectful actions and investing in myself. Dr. Joe Dispenza, immense respect. I hold many outstanding multidimensional memories. Caroline Myss, your 9 CD set "Entering the Castle" transformed me during M.E..

Last and not least, Jan Arriens, a new important friend in my life. I feel as if we have always known each other, and without knowing it your life was affecting my and Robert's lives, decades before we finally met. Intertwined destinies… Thank you for having had the passion, courage and inner power to found LifeLines.

As my spiritual journey continues, I want to acknowledge the people who have been there and helped me. Of course, first is Suzanne Michal. Although my spiritual journey began before we met, she has helped me to grow and continues to help me become a better person. Her friendship sustained me through the loss of my mother and grandmother.

To my daughter who helps me to have the will to continue fighting in this life and whose love and support continue to make me a stronger and better person and for giving me the privilege of being a father and grandfather.

My mother Novella, although my childhood was fret with abuse and trauma I want to thank her for the last years of her life, for allowing us to mend our relationship and for helping me to come to peace with my past.

As for people on the row, I want to acknowledge my friend Flip, who has helped me keep busy doing odd jobs and has never judged me for my mistakes. My "adopted brother" Gene who with his humor and knowledge has helped me through some trying times and who has never judged me for my past and my mistakes.

These people have contributed to me becoming who I am today, and I owe them my many thanks and love from the bottom of my heart.

Resources

Books mentioned:

Dreams of Awakening: Lucid Dreaming And Mindfulness Of Dream And Sleep; 2013 by C. Morley
Earth's Children; 1980 – 2011 by J.M. Auel
The Man in the Glass; 1934 by P.D. Wimbrow
Wishes Fulfilled: Mastering the Art of Manifesting; 2012, Dr. Wayne W. Dyer
Zero Limits: The Secret Hawaiian System for Wealth, Health, Peace, and More; 2008, by Joe Vitale, Ihaleakala Hew Len

Relevant websites:

Dr Joe Dispenza: www.drjoedispenza.com
Lifelines: www.lifelines-uk.org.uk
Joe Vitale: https://www.mrfire.com/
Dr Hew Len on Youtube and internet about his experiences on Ho'oponopono.
Jill Runnion spine healing: www.tetonsynapse.com
Endorphins meditation, William Bloom: www.williambloom.com
Heart coherence: www.heartmath.org
Suzanne's spiritual and energy work: www.daretoexpand.com
Death Café: www.deathcafe.com
Menopause Café: https://www.menopausecafe.net/
Lucid dreaming and more: https://www.charliemorley.com
Wayne Dyer: https://www.drwaynedyer.com and I highly recommend his film The Shift, on Youtube
Lightning Process: https://lightningprocess.co.uk/
Porter's testimonial:
https://www.youtube.com/watch?v=dIvP9lfFQWI

Table of Illustrations and Drawings

All illustrations are by Suzanne and all card drawings by Robert. All photographs of them were kindly taken by Sophie Gormand.

"Friends for Life", screen monoprint, joint portrait	vii
"Map of our Intention", sketched in 2017 as we were shaping the idea of the book, colour pencils	xv
"Robert, my Successful Co-Author", sketched as we were shaping the idea of the book, colour pencils	xvii
Suzanne's hands holding Robert's first letter	13
First card with Robert's variants on butterflies, black pen	25
"Punchy Message", black pen	56
"Symbol of Change", black pen	92
"Dirty Dishes Scene", colour pencils	102
"Symbol of Change", black pen	105
"In my Desigual Dress, Facing the Sun", colour pencils self-portrait	111
"French Bee Smelling Flowers", colour pencils self-portrait	131
"Couscous in our Garden Looking In", colour pencils	139
"Hoponopono Prayer", black pen	155
"Who have I Become?", colour pencils self-portrait	199
"Who has Robert Become?" colour pencils portrait	210

About the Authors

Suzanne Michal

Suzanne Michal is a creative, passionate woman who believes that true stories are the most powerful of all. And out of true stories, letters and diaries are the most poignant witnesses to someone's life.

She is a holistic therapist who aims to empower self-healing and self-mastering in her clients. She uses her gifts of hypersensitivity and intuition to inspire others on their own journey of evolution.

Suzanne is an artist who uses words, colours and shapes to convey emotional reactions about the importance of the present moment and a call for living in awareness and inner empowerment.

She lives in London with her beloved and they spend as much time as they can in nature.

www.daretoexpand.com

Robert Poyson #140419

"Who am I?" is a question Robert has asked himself more often than most of us.

In 2008, after ten years on death row, in solitary confinement, he woke up one day and looked in a mirror and he did not like what he saw. As he studied the person in the mirror, he remembered a poem he had memorized The Man In The Glass by Peter Dale Wimbrow Sr.

"When you get what you want in your struggle for self
And the world makes you king for a day
Just go to the mirror and look at yourself
And see what that man has to say.

For it isn't your father, or mother, or wife
Whose judgement upon you must pass
The fellow whose verdict counts most in your life
Is the one staring back from the glass.

He's the fellow to please – never mind all the rest
For he's with you, clear to the end
And you've passed your most difficult, dangerous test
If the man in the glass is your friend."

That day, Robert decided to change.

Robert has grown into a man of potent presence, full of compassion, humour and hope for humanity and the planet.

His wish is to have a voice in the world where his evolution despite many difficult and traumatic experiences, can help others find meaning and a deeper understanding of what it means to be truly a human being.

He is still waiting for execution.